MW01602094

ACT PREPARATION GUIDE

**The Ultimate Study Success Blueprint to Ace Your ACT
Exam & Land Your Dream College
Achieve a Top Score with Progress-Tracking Tools to
Master English, Math, Reading & Science**

Disclaimer

The materials and questions in this book have been carefully crafted by the author using a range of reputable educational sources, including ACT practice content. These have been adapted, modified, and tailored to align with the educational goals of this study guide.

It is important to note that, while every effort has been made to ensure the quality and accuracy of the content, it is not affiliated with or endorsed by ACT, Inc., the organization responsible for the ACT examination. Additionally, the questions and content in this study guide are not exact replicas of those found in the official ACT exam, and no guarantees are made regarding their similarity to actual exam questions.

Any resemblance between the content of this study guide and questions in official ACT exams is purely coincidental. The primary objective of this guide is to provide comprehensive practice and instructional material to aid students in their preparation for the ACT.

By using this study guide, readers acknowledge that the questions and materials are solely for educational purposes and are not intended to mirror the precise content of the ACT exam. The author and publisher accept no liability for any outcomes resulting from the use or misuse of the materials provided in this book.

Table of Contents

Introduction

Welcome to a new chapter on your path to academic success! You are holding a key that will open the doors to what you have always dreamed of.

By deciding to prepare, you are taking a step that will be definitive, you are walking toward the realization of your goals.

In the end, you will have a feeling of security; you will be completely ready to face one of the most important situations in your life.

I must clarify and make you aware that you will face more than a simple test; it is an opportunity to demonstrate your potential to face the challenges ahead.

Therefore, every time you start or retake a chapter of this guide you are investing in yourself, your dreams, your discipline, your management skills, and your mental strength.

I know very well that thinking about the future can cause you anxiety, but believe me, it is exciting to take the steps that will allow you to form yourself and reach new levels of growth.

Do the following exercise: Imagine the day you receive the acceptance letter; how would you feel? What feelings would you experience? What will that moment be like? I am sure it will be a moment full of pride and joy for you and yours.

Well, this guide will provide you with the necessary knowledge to maximize your chances of success, because this training you are about to begin goes beyond obtaining good results, it has to do with opening up a world of possibilities. Therefore, the tips I will present will help you overcome your limits and reach new heights.

To pass and achieve a good score you must know how to approach each question and develop skills beyond the ability to take a test.

My promise is that you will get useful knowledge for the rest of your life; you will learn how to analyze critically and have control under pressure, so I hope these pages encourage you to grow as a student and as a human being.

As for the test, which is the main reason why you are reading this guide, don't worry, because you will find specific content to train you. You will arrive at the test room and you will be there with full confidence because you will already know what to expect, how to face it with a proactive attitude and a winning strategy, and once you finish the test you will look back and feel proud of what you have achieved.

Today you begin to build a solid foundation to confront without problems the challenges that will come. The mere fact you are facing these pages means you have made a strong commitment, saying "yes" to your dreams, and "yes" to the dedication and hard work required to achieve them. If you maintain this attitude, each page you read and each exercise you complete will bring you closer to realizing your aspirations. Hard work will allow you to see the fruits in reality reflecting your full potential, and this will be just the beginning.

But I don't want you to get false ideas, or build a distorted reality, you have to know that the path is full of decisions, and choosing to train yourself is, without a doubt, one of those significant decisions. From this moment, you will discover a lot about yourself, your ability to persevere, and your determination. This process, in its entirety, will become a testimony of your potential to face and overcome the obstacles life presents.

This journey will fill you with conviction about yourself and will accompany you in many aspects, even during your university years. Whenever you feel it is difficult, you will remember that you are more than qualified.

I invite you to visualize, live, and feel the relief and satisfaction you will experience when you receive your grades, knowing you gave your best. The hours dedicated, the reviews, everything was worth it. Nothing can stop you when you are determined to build a bright future.

Many have already walked this path before and achieved great things. This guide you have in front of you has been a supportive resource for others, helping them accomplish their goal. They have found guidance and support here, equipping themselves to enjoy the difference between an average score and one that opens the doors to their dreams.

Reflect on this: What does it mean for you to face this test? What are your life aspirations? Do you want to complete one stage? Or do you want it to be transcendental for you?

If you aim to guarantee a great future, take this guide with a growth mindset. Understand and master each aspect, handling the methods for mathematical problems accurately. Keep in mind that the university will be more than a place to learn; it is an environment where you will grow and become the best version of yourself. Face what is to come with an expectant attitude and maintain that vision to avoid discouragement or giving up. There will be days when it feels exhausting and doubts arise. In those moments, remember why you started this path and what you want to achieve.

Soon, you'll be walking around campus, knowing all the effort and dedication were worth it. So, trust in your potential to grow.

Go ahead, your future awaits you!

I have already welcomed you and discussed what your future could look like if you take this step seriously and commit to training with this guide. In this preface, I want to focus on the introductory aspects. First, learn how to make the most of this guide.

How to Take Advantage of This Guide

Start by understanding its structure and how each part is designed to support you. It is divided into chapters that address different areas of knowledge necessary for your success. Each one is designed to teach and guide you to apply what you learn through simulated tests.

Familiarize yourself with the opening chapters. These will provide an overview of what is expected of you and how to organize yourself effectively. When you start, I suggest doing a self-assessment to identify what to improve. Here are tools to do it accurately. Use these resources to establish a clear baseline.

Each chapter focuses on a specific area: English, Mathematics, Reading, Science, and optional Writing. You will find a combination of detailed explanations, clear examples, and exercises, so don't just read the explanations; practice them.

The complete simulations included are invaluable tools. Treat them as if they were the real test by timing yourself and following all instructions precisely. After completing each one, review your work and use the explanations to understand your mistakes.

For greater benefit, follow a well-structured schedule. You will find suggestions for creating a plan that fits your other responsibilities. Set daily and weekly goals and adhere to them consistently.

An important part is management techniques that help you stay positive, which is essential for optimal performance. If at any point you feel confused, go back and review the relevant sections.

Introduction to the ACT (Historical Overview)

The story of the ACT began in 1959 when Everett Franklin Lindquist, a professor at the University of Iowa, envisioned creating an assessment as an alternative to the already established SAT. He believed a tool was needed that went beyond measuring just verbal and mathematical skills.

Lindquist, a pioneer in educational assessment, designed the ACT to be accessible and equitable for a diverse range of talents. Since its first administration in 1959, the ACT has undergone numerous transformations to adapt to changes in the educational system and societal needs. Initially, it focused on four main areas: English, Mathematics, Reading, and Science, providing a comprehensive view of academic abilities.

Over the decades, the ACT has been revised and updated to maintain relevance and accuracy. In 1989, changes were made to better reflect the secondary school curriculum and university expectations. Over time, the test continued to evolve with technological advances. In 2005, an optional writing section was added to address the growing importance of writing in higher education. This addition allowed participants to demonstrate their writing and argumentation abilities, adding another dimension to their academic profile.

Technological development has played a significant role in its constant transformation. In the last decade, a digital format was adopted, offering the option to take the test online. This transition has provided greater flexibility and accessibility, allowing students to perform in a more familiar and comfortable environment.

The organization behind the ACT has tirelessly worked to improve equity and accessibility. Various initiatives have been implemented to support low-income applicants and those with special needs, ensuring everyone has the opportunity to demonstrate their knowledge on equal terms.

The ACT's evolution has been guided by continuous research. Collaborations with educators and assessment experts have ensured it reflects best practices and aligns with the most recent standards. These efforts have led to constant improvements in quality and relevance, making the ACT a useful and accurate tool.

The ACT has played a crucial role in the lives of millions of young people, helping them access higher education. Its history is a testimony of the continuous commitment to excellence and equity. From its humble beginnings in Iowa, the ACT has grown to become one of the most recognized and respected assessments nationally.

Looking ahead, the ACT is far from over. Throughout its more than six decades of existence, it has proven to be a dynamic and adaptable tool, capable of evolving. The organization continues to explore new ways to improve and adapt the ACT to meet the changing needs of students and educational institutions.

Understanding the Structure of the ACT

To advance to the first chapter, you must understand how it works, its structure, and the scoring process.

The first is the English section. It consists of 75 multiple-choice questions to be completed in 45 minutes, divided into two main categories: Usage and Mechanics, which covers grammar and sentence structure, and Rhetorical Skills, which focuses on the organization and style of texts. It is scored on a scale of 1 to 36. There is no penalty for incorrect answers, so it is always advantageous to answer all questions.

The second is Mathematics, which includes 60 multiple-choice questions to be answered in 60 minutes. This section covers a wide range of topics, from basic algebra to trigonometry, and evaluates the ability to interpret graphs and apply mathematical concepts to various situations. Like the English section, it is scored from 1 to 36 based on the number of correct answers, with no penalty for incorrect ones. The total number of correct answers is converted to a scaled score.

The third is Reading, where you have 35 minutes to answer 40 multiple-choice questions. This section evaluates your ability to understand and interpret literary prose, humanities, social sciences, and natural sciences. Each passage is accompanied by questions that ask you to find the main ideas, specific details, inferences, and structure. This segment is also scored from 1 to 36.

The fourth is Science, with 40 multiple-choice questions to be completed in 35 minutes. This section does not directly measure your scientific knowledge but assesses your ability to interpret, analyze, and evaluate content of this type. The passages include tables and descriptions of experiments, and you will be asked to interpret data, compare hypotheses, and evaluate experimental results. It is scored from 1 to 36.

In addition to these sections, there is an optional writing part. If you decide to do it, you will have 40 minutes to write an essay. You must analyze a complex issue and develop a coherent and well-structured argument. This segment is evaluated based on your ability to generate ideas, organize content, use language, and support your argument with appropriate evidence. The writing is graded on a scale of 2 to 12 by two independent evaluators, each scoring from 1 to 6 in each domain, and their scores are combined.

The composite score is a general measure of your performance in all four main sections, calculated by averaging their scaled scores, and is typically considered in the admission process. In the same way, you will receive detailed evaluations in each section, which will help you identify your strengths and areas for improvement.

Now that you understand the preliminary issues, are you ready to move forward? If so, turn the page!

Part I:
Foundations for Success

Chapter 1: Setting the Stage

The first step in preparing for what could be your gateway to an extraordinary future is to set the stage. In this chapter, I will present the most fundamental aspects to give you a broader notion, making it easier to take the steps toward the future you desire and deserve.

You will find a segment detailing everything you need to do for admissions. This section provides a clear idea of the necessary steps, and I will explain how to set your goals in a way that keeps your motivation high. So, read and implement each of the following recommendations:

Understand the Importance of the ACT

Read and internalize these reasons why taking the ACT is necessary:

Admission Opportunities

Colleges receive thousands of applications each year, and a good score helps you stand out from other applicants. When reviewed by committees, a good score acts as a clear indicator, increasing your chances of acceptance. Higher education institutions seek students ready to succeed, and a good ACT score shows that you are one of them. This gives you more options, allowing you to apply to a broader range of schools, including those with higher requirements.

Eligibility for Scholarships and Financial Aid

Many universities offer performance-based scholarships that can ease the financial burden of college. These scholarships could cover part or all of your tuition and, in some cases, other expenses such as books, accommodation, and food. There are others awarded by external organizations, foundations, and companies that aim to support talented young people.

The government also offers financial aid partially based on ACT results, with some requiring a minimum score to be considered. Additionally, merit-based aid, unlike need-based aid, is awarded to those who demonstrate great potential, not just those who meet a minimum qualification.

Standard Comparison with Other Candidates

Since it represents a standardized measure for fair comparison, the ACT is an instrument you should take advantage of. High schools have different levels of academic rigor, and standardization allows all applicants to be evaluated under the same criteria, eliminating any differences between schools.

For you, this means your performance is evaluated equally, regardless of your educational background. If you have worked hard and performed well, the evaluation will place you in a favorable position compared to others.

Self-Discovery of Your Strengths

Knowing your strengths allows you to focus on developing them further, which is definitive for your success. If you score high in the Mathematics section, you will know you have strong analytical skills, and you might consider this when choosing a career.

Understanding what you are good at and what needs improvement helps you address your weaknesses more effectively. Preparing for the ACT forces you to confront and improve areas where you may not feel as confident.

Preparation for Future Tests

The preparation process teaches you how to organize yourself and develop essential skills for facing future challenges, such as more difficult and complex tests.

At this stage, you will develop skills to apply in your courses, enhancing your ability to understand and retain information. You will be able to tackle more complex materials and develop a deeper understanding of concepts. Continued practice and review help you see challenges as opportunities to improve.

The discipline and determination you cultivate will carry you through the next stages of your academic journey. You will be better equipped to handle the workload, easing your transition and improving your chances of success.

Enhancement of Your Confidence in Testing Skills

Every time you exercise and see improvements, your confidence grows. You no longer see tests as obstacles but as opportunities to demonstrate your knowledge. This level of security translates into greater peace of mind during the test, allowing you to think more clearly and respond more effectively.

Overcoming challenges during your preparation reinforces your resilience. You become accustomed to handling difficult situations and finding solutions, preparing you for any future assessment. You feel more confident participating in classes and presenting projects, more motivated to try harder, and make the most of the educational opportunities.

Flexibility in Submitting Scores to Various Institutions

You have the power to choose which scores to send to institutions that value them, increasing your chances of acceptance by projecting a completer and more favorable image of your abilities. If you have taken the test several times, select the highest scores from each section to send. This will make your profile more appealing and reflect your dedication and effort to improve, which is highly appreciated by the admissions committees.

This flexibility allows you to compare your scores with the requirements of different institutions. You can analyze each institution's expectations and strategically decide where to send your scores to maximize your chances of admission, always taking into account those that are most compatible with your profile.

The best point is that you are not restricted to a limited number of requests, allowing you to explore several options, including ones you may not have considered at the beginning.

Myths Related to the Test

Now you know why the ACT is a transcendental step, and before moving forward, it is necessary to demystify it, so you do not make mistakes. Read carefully and do not fall into believing these myths that could sabotage you even before presenting the test, leading you to obtain low scores:

Only Those with High Qualifications Achieve Good Results

This myth could discourage you if you don't have the best grades in your classes, making you believe there is no possibility of standing out. You might feel it is not worth trying, but the truth is it is not about being the best in all subjects; you must understand the format to feel comfortable.

Don't let this myth deprive you of the opportunity to demonstrate your true potential in a standardized environment.

You Need to Answer All the Questions Correctly

Thinking you must get them all right to succeed is another myth, and this adds unnecessary pressure, causing frustration and mental exhaustion.

It is enough to focus on answering as best as possible, without obsessing about perfection. That way, you will be more effective. Always keep in mind there is no penalty for incorrect answers, and in some cases, you could even guess. Thinking this way will reduce the pressure and help you arrive on test day with a more positive attitude and focus on progress.

Universities Only Consider the Composite Score

Many colleges look at grades separately to better understand your strengths and weaknesses.

If you excel in Mathematics but have difficulties in Reading, work on improving it. Keep in mind some institutions look for particular skills and pay more attention to one section than another.

You Can't Improve Much

This myth makes you feel resigned. The reality is very different: constant and strategic practice leads you to improve.

When you train, you become familiar with the format and details to take the test more efficiently. Each exercise allows you to correct mistakes.

A proactive attitude sees in each exercise and simulation a chance to learn. It will not be a mere task; it will transform your experience. Establish clear and measurable goals for each session, allowing you to monitor your progress and adjust as necessary. Don't worry! I will explain how to do it later.

Only Those in Certain Regions of the Country Take the ACT

t is common to believe that only those from certain regions of the country take the ACT, but the reality is young people from all over the United States, and even other countries, take it every year. The ACT is accepted by almost all universities and colleges in the country, making it a popular option in various geographical areas.

This false belief leads you to think it is not relevant if you live outside those supposed "specific regions." The availability of centers throughout the country makes it easy for anyone to access and participate, regardless of location. This accessibility means you can choose this test as a key part of your process, without worrying about being in a specific region.

The Test Is More Difficult Than Other Standardized Tests

Each test has its format and approach, so difficulty is perceived differently depending on individual strengths and weaknesses. The ACT includes Science, which is not present on the SAT, but this does not mean it is more difficult.

Your perception might depend on your familiarity with the format. If you are more accustomed to a standardized test, this one might seem more challenging at first.

However, the ACT covers what you have learned throughout high school. All parts of it are designed to test how ready you are, so don't be intimidated by the idea that it's harder than others. The difficulty is relative and you will overcome it.

Only Those Who Wish to Attend Specific Universities Should Take It

The reality is that taking the ACT benefits you no matter which schools you want to apply to, as many value it as part of the admission process.

And just as it is useful for educational institutions, it is useful for yourself, because it allows you to become aware of your capabilities. It gives you a precise measure of your level and what you should reinforce. In other words, it serves as an instrument to know where you might need to improve, giving you the chance to strengthen those aspects before starting your next stage.

Don't forget I mentioned it will help you obtain scholarships and other forms of financial aid.

Mathematics Requires Advanced Skills

The content in this section is designed to assess what you are expected to have learned during your high school years. Areas covered include algebra, geometry, trigonometry, and analysis, all topics that form part of the standard curriculum in most schools.

Therefore, believing this myth will lead you to feel intimidated for no reason. What you need is discipline in the weeks before the test to review. You do not require advanced knowledge outside the scope of the high school curriculum, but you do need a solid understanding of the concepts you have already seen in class.

Navigating College Admissions

Below are special recommendations to navigate this entire process successfully:

Investigate

Make a list of the areas you are passionate about and factors such as location, size of the university, and campus environment.

Use online resources such as websites, ratings, and forums to get an overview, and browse the pages on official sites.

Visit fairs to learn more about the schools that interest you and contact current students or alumni to get first-hand opinions about their experiences. It is helpful to review publications and articles about campus life and extracurricular opportunities.

I want to highlight the relevance of exploring the options for exchange programs and research opportunities available in each one because this enriches your education and gives you a ccmpetitive advantage in the future. Likewise, I recommend exploring housing options, since living on or off campus will influence your experience. Other aspects to take into account are the cost of living in different cities and how it will affect your budget, the quality, and availability of support services, such as tutoring, and counseling, among others, to select one that offers a quality education, and a supportive environment.

Within this phase, investigate retention and graduation rates, as these indicators reflect the level of satisfaction and success.

Understand Admission Requirements

Under the admissions tab on each option's official website, you'll find details on required documents, such as school transcripts, letters of recommendation, and personal essays.

Take note of the deadlines for submitting applications and have everything ready in advance. Make yourself a checklist to meet requirements and note the important dates so you can be organized and won't overlook any details.

If applicable, review the policies for people with special needs, consider the frequently asked questions on the pages, and even attend information sessions to clarify any doubts. If you have specific concerns, contact the office.

Make a Request Calendar

To do this, collect all the dates of each option you want to consider. Mark the deadlines for submission, both for regular admission and for early admission if you decide to opt for them. Include the dates for the standardized tests you need to take or resume, as well as the deadlines for sending the results.

Add the dates to recuest letters of recommendation from your professors, giving them enough time to write and send them. This calendar includes dates to work on your essay and review it several times, as well as the days to complete and verify online applications. Don't forget the deadlines to apply for scholarships and financial aid.

Break the process into manageable tasks and assign specific days to complete them. Review it frequently to adjust any dates that need to be reassigned and keep everything in one place.

Write a Strong Personal Essay

I have mentioned this to you in the previous steps, and now I want to explain how to do it correctly. Start by reflecting on your experiences, achievements, and aspirations. Think about the stories and moments that have shaped your life and could highlight your unique qualities. Choose a topic that is important to you and allows you to show your personality and unique perspective.

Draft your ideas without worrying about perfection, then review and edit them to improve coherence. Have a clear structure with an introduction that captures attention, a development that deepens your story, and a conclusion that summarizes your main message.

Use authentic and sincere language, avoiding clichés and generic phrases. Show your emotions and thoughts genuinely, and ensure your voice is heard. Ask people close to you to review it and offer constructive feedback.

Get Letters of Recommendation

Select teachers or mentors who know you well enough to discuss your strengths. They must have had a relationship with you, whether in the classroom, in extracurricular activities, or in specific projects. Ask them for this well in advance, at least a month before the deadline, so they have enough time to write a detailed and thoughtful letter.

It should highlight your achievements and character and include specific examples of your contributions in class, illustrating how you stand out among your peers. The letter should be sincere and personalized, avoiding generalities and focusing on what makes you unique. To achieve all this, those who recommend you should be able to talk in detail about each aspect. Share your resume and a summary of your achievements and aspirations with them. Inform them of the deadlines and submission procedures, and, if necessary, keep reminding them about it frequently and politely, to avoid being forgotten.

Complete the Application Accurately

When completing it, read all the instructions. Fill out each section carefully, and verify that your name, address, and contact information are correct and that the dates and everything about your previous education are accurate.

Avoid grammatical and spelling errors and proofread before sending. If you include open-ended questions, respond completely and thoughtfully.

Attach all necessary documents, such as transcripts, letters of recommendation, and essays, making sure they are in the indicated format and are legible. If there is an option to upload additional files that can strengthen your application, such as certificates of achievement or work samples, use it to present a more complete profile. Keep copies of everything sent for your records.

Admission Interviews

For this step, you should have already done the research. Review to refresh the mission, values, and what they are looking for, so you can respond and demonstrate your genuine interest. Prepare answers for the most common interview questions, such as why you chose that option, what your strengths and weaknesses are, and what motivates you to pursue your chosen career.

Prepare by visualizing it as a conversation where both parties know each other better. Relax and be yourself, showing authenticity, and working on your emotional component to manage your nerves, which you could achieve with deep breathing exercises and meditation.

On the day of the interview, dress appropriately to make a good impression. Wear professional and comfortable clothes, exercise your body language, and make eye contact.

Submit Standardized Test Scores

Access your account on the relevant website, such as ACT. Once logged in, select the option to send your scores and enter the specific codes of the institutions you have chosen. These codes are usually available on each institution's website.

Confirm that the scores you want to submit are correct, by selecting the highest ones from different dates that best represent you. Pay any fees associated with the submission, if necessary, and keep a copy of the receipt for your records.

After completing the process, verify that the scores have been received. If there is any delay, contact customer service to resolve it as soon as possible. Keep a record of all your transactions and correspondence for future reference.

Search and Apply for Scholarships and Financial Aid

Search scholarship databases, college websites, and local organizations offering financial support. Use keywords related to your interests and background to find specific options. You could even ask professors who might know of additional opportunities. Once you have selected your alternatives, review their requirements and verify that you meet the eligibility criteria before beginning the process. Gather all the necessary documents, such as transcripts, letters of recommendation, and essays. Personalize your applications for each scholarship, highlighting how you meet the requirements.

Complete the applications accurately, paying attention to deadlines. Keep a record of them, including submission dates and any correspondence. Always be persistent and look for new opportunities frequently.

Conduct Campus Visits

This part of the process is crucial because it allows you to experience the environment and culture firsthand. Confirm your visits in advance by contacting the admission offices to arrange tours and informational meetings. Research the campuses before your visit.

During your visit, explore the surroundings and facilities, residences, libraries, and common areas. Interact with students and staff to gain a genuine insight into campus life. Find out about the opportunities, extracurricular activities, and support services available.

If possible, participate in open classes to get an idea of the teaching style and academic level. Take notes on your impressions and reflect on how you would feel living and studying there.

Contact Admissions Officers

Write a clear and professional email introducing yourself and explaining your specific interests. Be concise and direct, avoiding unnecessary content. Ask questions about any opportunities on campus.

When communicating, avoid common mistakes such as being too informal or sending emails with grammatical and spelling errors. Proofread your messages before sending them.

Write in a respectful and professional tone and thank them for their assistance. If you have a phone conversation, prepare your questions beforehand and take notes during the call.

Now you just have to review all the admission offers you have received. Take into account the academic reputation of each institution and how their programs align with your interests. Review your campus visits and remember how you felt in each environment. Think about the conversations you had, and how you would fit into the community.

Do not forget to evaluate the extracurricular opportunities, the available resources, and the support offered for development. Similarly, measure and calculate all the financial aspects, such as the cost of tuition, scholarships, and financial aid that you have been offered. Analyze how these factors will impact your daily life and long-term well-being.

Goal Setting and Motivation

With these steps, your goals will be powerful and achievable. They will keep you motivated at each stage:

Define Specific Objectives

It is not enough to say "I want to improve;" instead, set a clear goal like "I want to get 30 points in math." This specificity allows you to create a more focused and efficient plan. The same applies to your educational future, in general; it is not enough to say "I want to pursue higher education." You must determine which ones you want to apply for and what you are interested in. You could say "I want to be admitted to Stanford University's Engineering program," so you can define exactly what steps you must take and what requirements you must meet.

Clarity gives you a series of advantages. You will be able to discover the resources you need to achieve your goals, what you need to reinforce, and how to structure your efforts. This approach helps you measure your progress and adjust your efforts accordingly. I will discuss this later before finishing this chapter.

All of this, in addition to being motivating, is very useful because it gives you a detailed map. Each effort you make will be aligned with a clear and concrete purpose, increasing your chances of success.

Make Sure Your Goals Are Measurable

If your goals are not measurable, it will be difficult for you to know if you are making progress or how far you are from reaching them, and this becomes the perfect condition for frustration and demotivation to arise. To achieve this, define specific criteria allowing you to evaluate your success, put a number you want to achieve, and each time you run a simulation, compare your current results to your goal to see how much you need to get there.

This allows you to set milestones and reward yourself when you reach each one. By knowing exactly how close you are, you have the information to adjust your efforts more effectively. Thus, every step you take brings you closer and motivates you on your academic path.

Set Realistic Deadlines

When you define achievable deadlines, you reduce the likelihood of feeling distressed and avoid burnout. Be honest about how much you need to improve. If you want to increase in a specific section, determine how much you will dedicate to it each day without affecting other responsibilities. By doing so, you establish a deadline respecting your daily rhythm of life.

Knowing you have a specific schedule forces you to be better organized and more efficient. It gives you better conditions to organize regular sessions, divide your process into manageable stages, and cover all the necessary material without feeling rushed.

Each time you achieve one objective on schedule, your confidence increases, motivating you to keep going. This positive cycle of establishment and fulfillment reinforces your ability to handle future challenges.

Break Down Your Goals into Small, Manageable Steps

This division makes each one seem less intimidating and more achievable, allowing you to focus on one thing at a time, thus being able to discover and correct specific problems more effectively. If you find difficulties with a particular topic, you could dedicate more time to it, without feeling like you are delaying all your progress.

This would be one way how to do it: review basic algebra concepts for a week; the next week, practice advanced algebra problems; and then move on to geometry. This step-by-step helps you build a solid foundation before moving on to more complex topics. It gives you a structured and manageable process, where each step brings you closer to what you want to achieve.

Prioritize Your Goals According to Their Importance

Evaluate each one based on its long-term impact and relevance. To assign a level of priority, take into account the upcoming deadlines, how each one contributes to your goals, and how much effort they will require.

Think about the value it will add to your development. Goals providing you with transferable skills or improving your academic profile should receive a higher preference, but you should always be flexible and willing to adjust your priorities.

Write Your Goals in a Visible Place

This is a way to stay focused and motivated. By seeing them every day, you reinforce your commitment and remember what you are working to achieve.

Place them where you will see them frequently, such as on your desk, on the wall of your room, or on your daily agenda. These help you keep them present, which facilitates perseverance and constant monitoring.

There are other ways to keep them visible, such as creating a vision board with images and inspirational quotes representing your goals, setting digital reminders on your phone or computer to appear at key times of the day, using tracking apps to record your progress, and receiving notifications keeping on track.

Monitor Your Progress

Frequent monitoring will help you detect any deviation and make the necessary adjustments. For this, a good system will be useful. First of all, define clear indicators allowing you to evaluate your progress. The good news is that if your goals have been established in a measurable, realistic way and you have divided them into small and manageable steps, with a good level of priority for each one, then you will have a good series of indicators. Organize a calendar, whether in a notebook, a spreadsheet, or a tracking application and make a note of the dates on which you would like to evaluate your progress and the criteria you will use to do so. Be consistent in the periodicity; decide if you will do it weekly, biweekly, or monthly.

Adjust Your Goals as Necessary

Sometimes circumstances change, or you encounter unexpected challenges requiring modifications. To do this, honestly evaluate your progress and the difficulties you have encountered and reflect on what aspects are not working and why. If necessary, redefine your goal to make it even more realistic and manageable. If you want to improve on all sections of the ACT in a short time, adjust your deadlines or focus on improving one at a time.

Consult with mentors, counselors, or people you trust to get an outside perspective. Sometimes other people may give you ideas and solutions you have not considered. Based on what you have discovered, adapt your strategies and establish new specific actions to help you overcome obstacles.

Chapter 2: Developing an Effective Study Plan

You already have the scenario established, and it is the first step to moving toward success. Now it is time to develop a plan, you must understand a series of fundamental aspects. This is why, in this chapter, I will present the benefits so you will have greater awareness about why to plan. You will discover the mistakes to avoid being effective, learn how to position yourself and be aware of the moment you are in to organize your future steps. I provide you in this chapter with two templates that will serve to guide you, and at the end, a reflection to encourage you to have a good balance in your plan.

Benefits of Having a Plan

Next, keep in mind these benefits which should become motivation to move forward:

Better Organization

When you organize yourself well, you are more likely to allocate specific periods for review and other activities. By knowing when to engage in each, you maintain a healthy balance, improving your overall well-being.

Organization maximizes your efficiency. You don't waste hours deciding what to do next, because you already have a pre-established schedule guiding you through each day. This helps you develop a distraction-free approach, making the most of each session and enjoying the feeling of accomplishment you get from completing each aspect.

On the other hand, it is easier to adapt to unexpected changes, keeping the rhythm, and remain productive even in difficult situations.

Greater Focus on Areas That Need Improvement

When you focus your efforts where you struggle most, you specifically address your weaknesses and are more likely to turn them into strengths.

Instead of distributing your efforts evenly, you prioritize the subjects or topics requiring the most attention, so you can be sure that you are working strategically to close the gaps in your knowledge, leading to faster progress.

Stress Reduction

When you feel distressed, it is difficult to concentrate, and if this is constant, it generates mental fatigue, making it difficult to think clearly, not to mention the physical consequences, such as headaches, digestive problems, and a weakened immune system.

On a mental level, it makes it feel like a burden and not an opportunity. This results in underperformance, intensifying stress, and making you feel lost in the amount of material you need to cover.

Productivity Increase

The lack of a concrete route leads you to procrastination. Without direction, it's easy to spend hours without a clear focus, resulting in superficial coverage of topics, leaving you with gaps.

With a clear guide, each session has a defined purpose and encourages you to move forward. You have a system to check each aspect, each step, and fulfilling it motivates you to maintain your productivity. This way, without being burdensome, you will have covered more material with greater depth.

Improved Retention

When you do not remember what you have read or practiced, your efforts become useless, and that happens when your moments are disorganized and dispersed because it makes it difficult to consolidate the content in your memory. You end up forgetting details and without a clear understanding of the key concepts.

Constant repetition allows you to move information from short-term to long-term memory. Divide the material into manageable sessions and assign periodic reviews, giving you the confidence to retain it.

On the other hand, you are more likely to use mind maps, flashcards, and summaries, which improve retention, focusing on the ones working best for you, and optimizing your ability to remember critical concepts.

Effective Habits

With a plan you avoid negative habits, establish specific schedules, avoid burnout, and improve your focus, all thanks to the possibility of having shorter and more frequent deadlines.

Positive habits include organization, consistency, and regular review, which create conditions to adjust as necessary.

Balance With Other Activities

If you only focus on studying, you could burn out quickly, which decreases your ability to stay motivated. On the other hand, neglecting your studies to carry out other activities also impairs your preparation.

To better organize yourself, establish a schedule including review and recreational activities and rest. You could review in the morning and dedicate the afternoon to hobbies or meetings with friends and family.

Having space in your assigned schedule to relax, you can concentrate better, knowing you will be able to enjoy other things. This balanced criterion improves both your learning and your mental and physical well-being.

Increase in Academic Self-Confidence

When you feel confident in your abilities, you are more willing to face challenges and persevere in the face of difficulties because you believe in your capacity to understand and master the material.

A schedule, a timeline, and a calendar are resources that give you a sense of control and purpose, allowing you to focus on your goals. Each time you complete a task, your confidence increases, reinforcing your belief in your ability to achieve your goals. This translates into better performance in the simulations and on the ACT itself.

Without this quality, it is easy to become distressed by the amount of material and expectations, resulting in underperformance.

Mistakes to Avoid

If you avoid mistakes, you will achieve greater effectiveness:

Not Considering Personal Learning Style

This is necessary to maximize your study sessions. You could be a visual learner, who retains better through graphs, diagrams, and videos, or perhaps an auditory one, who benefits more from listening to lectures or discussing topics out loud, or you could be kinesthetic, who assimilates better through movement.

Reflect on how you have learned best in the past. Experiment and see which methods help you understand and retain information better.

If you don't, you will end up with less productive and more frustrating sessions. If you are a visual learner and struggle with long readings without any visual support, you might find it hard to remember information.

Not Integrating Active Learning

This involves you in the process, making you actively participate in the acquisition of knowledge. You could try discussing topics with others, teaching concepts to someone else, or using flashcards to review. These methods promote a deep and lasting understanding of the material and go beyond just passive memorization.

If you don't integrate active learning, you will likely forget information and have difficulty applying what you have learned.

Neglecting Mental and Emotional Preparation

To succeed in this test, you need to see challenges as opportunities to improve. This helps you maintain perseverance and a healthy balance between study and rest.

Practice meditation and deep breathing, and establish routines that include space for self-care, so you can have a balanced emotional state.

Not Scheduling Reflections

If you do not reflect, you could miss the opportunity to consolidate and understand the concepts.

Reflection allows you to review and analyze areas that need more attention and reinforce what you have already learned. Without this, it's easy for information to dissipate and not be fully integrated into your long-term memory.

Write down the key concepts and think about how they relate to other topics. Ask yourself if there is something you still don't understand and write it down to review later.

Excluding the Use of Multimedia Resources

This exclusion makes your effort less effective and more boring. Multimedia resources, such as educational videos, podcasts, infographics, and interactive applications, offer various ways to present and explain information. These elements make complex concepts more accessible and easier to understand, especially if you are visual or auditory.

Including them allows you to approach the material from different angles. Watching an explanatory video on a difficult topic gives you a new perspective, and these resources make learning more dynamic and attractive, maintaining your interest and motivation.

To integrate them, you could search for educational videos on platforms like YouTube, use apps that offer interactive exercises, and listen to podcasts that discuss relevant topics.

Not Balancing Theory with Implementation

Focusing only on theory causes you to memorize concepts without understanding how to use them in real situations. This becomes a problem when you face questions requiring the implementation of those concepts.

To create balance, integrate exercises along with theory. After studying a concept, such as mathematics, complete practice problems after reviewing the formulas and concepts. You should practice speaking and writing when learning a new language, but avoid memorizing vocabulary and grammar.

Not Creating a Suitable Environment

To create a good environment, choose a quiet place free of distractions, well-lit, and with a comfortable temperature, with all the necessary materials within reach, such as books, notebooks, and electronic devices. Eliminate any potential distractions, such as mobile devices or televisions.

Personalize your space with items that motivate you, such as inspirational quotes. You should also have an ergonomic chair and desk.

Evaluate Your Starting Criteria

To do this, you need a clear understanding of your current skills and what you need to improve. This will allow you to focus your efforts more effectively and ensure you are making progress toward your goals.

Start by examining your academic performance so far, looking at your grades, teachers' comments, and any assessments you have completed. This will give you a clear idea of your strengths and weaknesses. With this analysis, you can discover patterns and trends that might not be obvious to the naked eye.

Reflect on how you feel when studying each subject. Are there topics that are difficult for you? Are there areas where you feel confident and enjoy the most?

Take into account your current habits. Do you prefer to do it in the morning or at night? Do you retain information better during long study sessions or shorter intervals? Examine your techniques: Do you use summaries, flashcards, and group discussions, or do you prefer to study alone? Understanding your current methods allows you to know what is working well and what needs to change.

Another powerful tool is performing self-assessments or diagnoses. Many online resources offer quizzes to test your knowledge, giving you an objective measure of your current skill level and helping you discover gaps. After completing a simulation, consider what area you need to improve.

Keep in mind your goals and how they align with your current abilities. If you want to get into a prestigious university requiring high standardized test scores, evaluate how close you are to achieving them.

Management is another factor. Although I will discuss this in more detail later, I want you to have an idea of how to evaluate your management. Do you spend enough hours reviewing each subject? Do you balance well with other responsibilities? Keeping track of these aspects for at least a week will reveal where you might be wasting daily hours and how you could redistribute them more efficiently.

Motivation and personal discipline are also crucial in determining your progress. Reflect on your level of enthusiasm and your ability to stay focused. Do you find it easy to follow a schedule, or are you easily distracted?

By examining these aspects, you will be able to determine how to establish a schedule to prepare for the test, marking the beginning of a new stage in your life. You will get a complete vision of your current situation, increasing your chances of success and giving you the necessary push to keep going.

Create a Schedule

With all the knowledge that I have shared with you in this chapter, you now know how to start creating your schedule. You could organize a general monthly schedule and another more specific one that addresses each day of the week.

Below, I share two templates to guide you:

Template for a Monthly Schedule

Month: [Name of the month]

Week 1

Goal of the week: Review fundamental concepts and establish a solid foundation in key areas.

Monday:

- **Mathematics:** Basic Algebra
- **English:** Grammar and Usage

Tuesday:

- **Sciences:** Scientific Methods
- **Passage Comprehension**

Wednesday:

- **Mathematics:** Geometry
- **English:** Essay Writing

Thursday:

- **Science:** Graph Interpretation
- **Critical Reading:** Analysis

Friday:

- Mathematics: Functions
- English: Grammar

Saturday:

- **Simulation of Previous Exams:** Mathematics and Science
- **Review:** Problem Areas

Sunday:

- **Rest and Recreational Activities**
- **Next Week's Schedule**

Week 2

Goal of the week: Delve into intermediate topics and reinforce problem-solving skills.

Monday:

- **Mathematics:** Trigonometry
- **English:** [Specify Topic]

Tuesday:

- **Science:** Data Interpretation
- **Passage Comprehension**

Wednesday:

- **Mathematics:** Advanced Algebra
- **English:** Essay

Thursday:

- **Science:** Analysis of Experiments
- **Critical Reading:** Analysis

Friday:

- **Mathematics:** Statistics
- **English:** Grammar

Saturday:

- **Simulation of Previous Exams:** English and Science
- **Review:** Problem Areas

Sunday:

- **Rest and Recreational Activities**
- **Next Week's Schedule**

Week 3

Goal of the week: Apply knowledge in test situations and improve.

Monday:

- **Mathematics:** Application
- **English:** [Specify Topic]

Tuesday:

- **Science:** Advanced Table Interpretation
- **Critical Reading:** Advanced Understanding

Wednesday:

- **Mathematics:** Complex Problems
- **English:** Essay

Thursday:

- **Sciences:** Tables
- **Critical Reading:** Analysis

Friday:

- **Mathematics:** General Review
- **English:** Advanced Simulation

Saturday:

- **Complete Drill**
- **Review and Analysis of the Drill**

Sunday:

- **Rest and Recreational Activities**
- **Next Week's Schedule**

Week 4

Goal of the week: Consolidate and carry out intensive practices.

Monday:

- **Mathematics:** General Review
- **English:** Writing and Grammar

Tuesday:

- **Science:** Review of Key Topics
- **Critical Reading:** Intensive Review

Wednesday:

- **Mathematics:** Review of Difficult Problems
- **English:** Final Practice Essay

Thursday:

- **Science:** Final Practice
- **Critical Reading:** Final Practice

Friday:

- **Mathematics:** Review of Difficult Topics
- **English:** Final Adjustments

Saturday:

- **Complete Drill**
- **Review and Final Adjustment**

Sunday:

- Rest

Template for a Daily Schedule

This will work for you; you just have to change according to your criteria:

Week from: [Start Date] to [End Date]

Monday

- 6:30 AM - 7:00 AM: Breakfast
- 7:00 AM - 8:00 AM: Mathematics (Algebra)
- 8:00 AM - 9:00 AM: Other Commitments (classes/work)
- 9:00 AM - 10:00 AM: Other Commitments (classes/work)
- 10:00 AM - 11:00 AM: English (Grammar and Usage)
- 11:00 AM - 12:00 PM: Other Commitments (classes/work)
- 12:00 PM - 1:00 PM: Lunch and Rest
- 1:00 PM - 2:00 PM: Science (Interpretation of Diagrams)
- 2:00 PM - 3:00 PM: Other Commitments (classes/work)
- 3:00 PM - 4:00 PM: Other Commitments (classes/work)
- 4:00 PM - 5:00 PM: Passages and Understanding
- 5:00 PM - 6:00 PM: Free (Hobbies)
- 6:00 PM - 7:00 PM: Dinner

- 7:00 PM - 8:00 PM: Practice of Previous Exams (Mathematics)
- 8:00 PM - 9:00 PM: Relaxation
- 9:00 PM - 10:00 PM: Light Review and Programming for the Next Day

Tuesday

- 6:30 AM - 7:00 AM: Breakfast
- 7:00 AM - 8:00 AM: Mathematics (Geometry)
- 8:00 AM - 9:00 AM: Other Commitments (classes/work)
- 9:00 AM - 10:00 AM: Other Commitments (classes/work)
- 10:00 AM - 11:00 AM: English
- 11:00 AM - 12:00 PM: Other Commitments (classes/work)
- 12:00 PM - 1:00 PM: Lunch and Rest
- 1:00 PM - 2:00 PM: Science (Graph Interpretation)
- 2:00 PM - 3:00 PM: Other Commitments (classes/work)
- 3:00 PM - 4:00 PM: Other Commitments (classes/work)
- 4:00 PM - 5:00 PM: Mathematics (Trigonometry)
- 5:00 PM - 6:00 PM: Free (Hobbies)
- 6:00 PM - 7:00 PM: Dinner
- 7:00 PM - 8:00 PM: Practice of Previous Exams
- 8:00 PM - 9:00 PM: Relaxation
- 9:00 PM - 10:00 PM: Light Review and Programming for the Next Day

Wednesday

- 6:30 AM - 7:00 AM: Breakfast
- 7:00 AM - 8:00 AM: Mathematics (Functions)
- 8:00 AM - 9:00 AM: Other Commitments (classes/work)
- 9:00 AM - 10:00 AM: Other Commitments (classes/work)
- 10:00 AM - 11:00 AM: English (Grammar and Usage)
- 11:00 AM - 12:00 PM: Other Commitments (classes/work)

- 12:00 PM - 1:00 PM: Lunch and Rest
- 1:00 PM - 2:00 PM: Sciences (Scientific Methods)
- 2:00 PM - 3:00 PM: Other Commitments (classes/work)
- 3:00 PM - 4:00 PM: Other Commitments (classes/work)
- 4:00 PM - 5:00 PM: Critical Reading (Analysis)
- 5:00 PM - 6:00 PM: Free (Hobbies)
- 6:00 PM - 7:00 PM: Dinner
- 7:00 PM - 8:00 PM: Practice of Previous Exams (Science)
- 8:00 PM - 9:00 PM: Relaxation
- 9:00 PM - 10:00 PM: Light Review and Programming for the Next Day

Thursday

- 6:30 AM - 7:00 AM: Breakfast
- 7:00 AM - 8:00 AM: Mathematics (Algebra)
- 8:00 AM - 9:00 AM: Other Commitments (classes/work)
- 9:00 AM - 10:00 AM: Other Commitments (classes/work)
- 10:00 AM - 11:00 AM: English (Essay Writing)
- 11:00 AM - 12:00 PM: Other Commitments (classes/work)
- 12:00 PM - 1:00 PM: Lunch and Rest
- 1:00 PM - 2:00 PM: Science (Interpretation of Experiments)
- 2:00 PM - 3:00 PM: Other Commitments (classes/work)
- 3:00 PM - 4:00 PM: Other Commitments (classes/work)
- 4:00 PM - 5:00 PM: Passages and Understanding
- 5:00 PM - 6:00 PM: Free (Hobbies)
- 6:00 PM - 7:00 PM: Dinner
- 7:00 PM - 8:00 PM: Practice of Previous Exams (English)
- 8:00 PM - 9:00 PM: Relaxation
- 9:00 PM - 10:00 PM: Light Review and Programming for the Next Day

Friday

- 6:30 AM - 7:00 AM: Breakfast
- 7:00 AM - 8:00 AM: Mathematics (Algebra and Trigonometry)
- 8:00 AM - 9:00 AM: Other Commitments (classes/work)
- 9:00 AM - 10:00 AM: Other Commitments (classes/work)
- 10:00 AM - 11:00 AM: English (Grammar and Usage)
- 11:00 AM - 12:00 PM: Other Commitments (classes/work)
- 12:00 PM - 1:00 PM: Lunch and Rest
- 1:00 PM - 2:00 PM: Science (Table Analysis)
- 2:00 PM - 3:00 PM: Other Commitments (classes/work)
- 3:00 PM - 4:00 PM: Other Commitments (classes/work)
- 4:00 PM - 5:00 PM: Critical Reading (Analysis)
- 5:00 PM - 6:00 PM: Free (Hobbies)
- 6:00 PM - 7:00 PM: Dinner
- 7:00 PM - 8:00 PM: Practice of Previous Exams (Mathematics)
- 8:00 PM - 9:00 PM: Relaxation
- 9:00 PM - 10:00 PM: Light Review and Programming for the Next Day

Saturday

- 8:00 AM - 9:00 AM: Mathematics (General Review)
- 9:00 AM - 10:00 AM: English
- 10:00 AM - 10:15 AM: Rest (Stretching and Deep Breathing)
- 10:15 AM - 11:15 AM: Science (Analysis)
- 11:15 AM - 12:15 PM: Free (Recreational Activity)
- 12:15 PM - 1:15 PM: Lunch
- 1:15 PM - 2:15 PM: Writing (Rehearsal)
- 2:15 PM - 3:15 PM: General Review
- 3:15 PM - 4:00 PM: Free (Relaxation)

- 4:00 PM - 5:00 PM: Review of Problem Areas

Sunday

- Rest and Recreational Activities
- Next Week's Schedule
- Light Review and Mental Preparation for the Week

Balance ACT Preparation with Other Responsibilities

It might seem like a difficult challenge, almost impossible; but consider the tips you have read in the chapter, and you must start from all your current responsibilities, such as your classes, extracurricular activities, perhaps a part-time job, and also, your active social life.

To start, make a schedule based on your plan. You already have templates for this and specific guidelines. With a clear overview, book specific blocks that should be consistent and fit into your daily routine. If you have classes during the day, it is more effective to study in the afternoon or at night.

Be realistic about how much you have without compromising your other responsibilities, and do not make the mistake, which I have already told you about, of spending endless hours in front of books. Instead, do it intelligently and efficiently. Set daily or weekly goals to have better conditions to measure your progress. If one day you only have the availability to dedicate an hour, just do it in a productive way and free of distractions.

If you take the bus to school, review flashcards, or listen to educational podcasts on the way. Take advantage of the small free moments to do quick reviews; these intervals add up and make a big difference without feeling like you are sacrificing other activities.

Be flexible to handle multiple responsibilities. There will be days when unforeseen events or last-minute commitments interrupt your schedule. Instead of stressing about missing a session, adjust your calendar and find another time. I recommend that you explain to your teachers and coaches that you are preparing for the ACT to support or adjust your assignments. Most of them understand the importance and will be willing to help you find a balance.

The support of family and friends will be decisive. Talk to them about your goals and your schedule. In this sense, form groups with classmates who are in the same situation. This makes learning more interactive and less solitary, and everyone will be able to benefit from the strategies together.

Achieving balance is a challenge, but it will be possible for you if you take into account everything you have discovered in this chapter. Just find a rhythm that works for you, stay organized, and be consistent.

Chapter 3: Test-Taking Strategies and Mindset

If you have made it this far, you are already familiar with the fundamentals, and this is a big step forward.

This chapter continues to be part of the foundations on which you must start to be successful in this significant milestone, which will mark your future. It is dedicated to mental keys so neither anxiety nor nerves nor any other emotion sabotages you. So read very carefully and with the willingness to implement everything you will discover below:

Managing Test Anxiety

Anxiety is a natural reaction of the body to situations perceived as threatening or stressful. It is a feeling of worry, nervousness, or fear about future events, particularly those that are challenging or unknown. It is common to experience this phenomenon due to the pressure and expectations to get a good rating. It may well happen even when you feel ready because uncertainty and the desire to succeed intensify your emotions.

Now, you should know the origin of anxiety is in the nervous system, in a part of the brain called the amygdala, which processes emotions and detects threats. When you perceive a stressful situation, it sends signals to your body for fight or flight, triggering the release of hormones such as cortisol and adrenaline, which increase your heart rate, speed up your breathing, and put your body on high alert. Although it is useful in situations of physical danger, it is less beneficial when you are facing an exam, as it makes it difficult to concentrate.

So, you need to determine the potential causes, and of course, the first one in this scenario could be academic pressure. As a high school student, you may feel your future depends on your performance on the ACT, not to mention the expectations of your parents, teachers, and yourself. Other potential causes include fear of failure and comparison with others. Your classmates increase your level of nervousness. If when the day comes you feel like you haven't reviewed enough or don't fully understand the material, it's natural to feel restless. The uncertainty about what to expect and the worry of not being ready intensify anxiety, especially if you have had previous negative experiences with other tests because you may associate those emotions with the current situation.

Other causes are considered external factors and could be linked to your context; some are personal, family, or social problems.

All the factors mentioned so far, and even imagining negative situations on the day of the test, generate constant worry, making it difficult for you to concentrate. You will feel restless because you are busy with negative thoughts, and your memory and ability to remember will be affected.

Avoidance behavior is another common manifestation; you will be tempted to procrastinate or avoid studying completely because every time you try, you feel stressed. This avoidance creates a negative cycle where you feel more nervous because you are not studying, which in turn makes you avoid it even more. When this situation continues, your quality-of-life decreases, and you will feel irritated or depressed, which affects your relationships with friends and family.

Recognizing that this sensation is natural that and everyone experiences it at some point is the first step to facing it with a more positive perspective. Knowing it is a biological reaction to situations, perceived as threatening, alleviates part of the fear, and knowing the causes is the key. The second step is to take control and address anxiety more strategically.

Develop a routine that allows you to face it proactively, including relaxation and mindfulness to calm yourself. But don't worry, on the following pages, you will find a series of strategies to experiment with and find the one that best suits you:

Biofeedback With Heart Rate Monitoring

It allows you to observe and control your physiological reactions to reduce stress. Use devices that record your vital signs and give you instant feedback:

1. Place the monitoring device on your finger or wrist.

2. Watch the screen to see your heart rate.

3. Breathe, inhaling through your nose and exhaling through your mouth.

4. Try to align your breathing with a constant rhythm, for example, four seconds to inhale and four seconds to exhale.

5. Notice how your heart rate changes as you maintain this controlled breathing.

6. If your heart rate slows, continue breathing steadily and deeply.

7. If it doesn't slow down, try adjusting your pace until you find one that works better.

8. Practice it for five to ten minutes a day to become familiar with the process.

Jacobson's Progressive Muscle Relaxation

It consists of tensing and relaxing different muscle groups in the body. This is how you can release physical and mental tension, reducing stress and anxiety:

1. Tense the muscles in your feet and hold the tension for five seconds.

2. Relax them and feel the tension melt away.

3. Move to your calf muscles, and tense for five seconds.

4. Relax them and notice the difference in sensation.

5. Continue with your thigh muscles, tensing them for five seconds.

6. Relax them and see what relaxation feels like.

7. Repeat this process with each muscle group, moving up the body, until you reach those in the neck and face.

Guided Visualization

This technique helps strengthen your mental resilience and reduce stress:

1. Close your eyes and take a deep breath.

2. Imagine walking into the exam room, feeling calm.

3. Visualize receiving the test and knowing how to respond.

4. Imagine yourself writing the answers confidently and accurately.

5. Go through each section, completing it without rushing.

6. Visualize finishing, handing in your test, and feeling satisfied with your performance.

Grounding

This method helps anchor you in the present, using your five senses to reduce anxiety and improve focus.

1. Look around you and name five things you can see.

2. Locate four things you can touch.

3. Listen carefully and mention three things you can hear.

4. Focus on two things you can smell.

5. Notice one thing you can taste.

6. Breathe deeply and feel your body relax.

7. Review each thing you named, appreciating their presence.

Systematic Desensitization

This technique reduces fear or anxiety by exposing yourself to the source of your stress in a controlled manner:

1. Identify the specific aspects that cause you the most stress.

2. Imagine the least stressful related situation.

3. Visualize it until you feel relaxed and comfortable.

4. Move on to a slightly more stressful situation, like the day before the test, and repeat the visualization until you feel relaxed.

5. Continue exposing yourself to stressful situations, such as entering the room and receiving the test.

6. Practice daily, gradually increasing the level of stress.

7. Once comfortable with all the situations, repeat the process frequently to maintain your level of relaxation.

Mindfulness With Focus on Breathing

This method focuses on breathing to stay present and reduce stress:

1. Take a deep breath, inhaling through your nose and exhaling through your mouth.

2. Focus on the sensation of the air entering and leaving your lungs.

3. Count each inhalation and exhalation from one to ten; then, start over.

4. Continue for several minutes, allowing any thoughts or worries to fade as you focus on your breathing.

Using a Stress Ball During Anxious Times

This technique helps release accumulated physical and mental tension:

1. Hold the stress ball in your dominant hand.

2. Squeeze the ball hard for about five seconds.

3. Release the pressure, allowing your hand to relax completely.

4. Repeat the squeeze and release several times.

5. Focus on the sensation of the ball and each squeeze.

6. Adjust the intensity depending on what feels most relaxing.

Emotional Freedom Technique (EFT)

This method combines acupressure and psychology to release emotional blockages:

1. Identify the specific source of your anxiety.

2. Rate the intensity of your discomfort on a scale of 1 to 10.

3. While you focus on the sensation, use two fingers to gently tap the outside edge of your hand.

4. Repeat an affirmative phrase, such as "Even though I feel stressed, I completely accept and forgive myself."

5. Move the taps to other points: between the eyebrows, next to the eye, under the eye, under the nose, on the chin, on the collarbone, and under the arm.

6. Repeat the affirmative phrase or a variation at each point.

7. After completing the sequence, evaluate the intensity of your discomfort.

8. If it is still high, repeat the tapping sequence.

Listen to Binaural Music to Reduce Stress

It uses different frequencies in each ear to induce relaxation:

1. Put on headphones and select a binaural music track designed for relaxation.

2. Adjust the volume to a comfortable, non-distracting level.

3. Close your eyes and focus on the differences in sound between the two ears.

4. Focus on the sound waves, letting stressful thoughts fade away.

5. Listen for at least ten minutes to maximize benefits.

Therapeutic Writing of Thoughts and Concerns

This method is used to release emotional tension and clarify your thoughts:

1. Take a notebook and a pen.

2. Write down any thoughts or concerns you have.

3. Don't worry about grammar or spelling; just write freely.

4. Review what you have written and reflect on your concerns.

5. If you find a solution, write it down.

Cognitive Restructuring to Challenge Negative Thoughts

It helps change negative and distorted thoughts:

1. Determine a recurring negative thought, such as "I'm going to fail."

2. Question its veracity: Is it true? Is there evidence to support it?

3. Look for evidence contradicting the thought: Have you succeeded on previous tests?

4. Replace it with a more positive and realistic one, such as "I have studied and am prepared to do well."

5. Practice repeating the new thought every time the negative one appears.

Tai Chi Exercises to Reduce Physical and Mental Tension

This Chinese practice combines gentle movements with deep breathing and meditation:

1. Start standing with your feet shoulder-width apart, knees slightly bent, and arms relaxed.

2. Inhale as you raise your arms in front of you to shoulder height.

3. Exhale as you lower your arms back to your sides.

4. Imagine holding a large, heavy ball, and gently moving it from side to side.

5. Shift your weight from one foot to the other as you swing your arms from side to side, keeping movements slow and controlled.

6. Twist your torso with each movement, keeping your spine straight.

7. Continue synchronizing your breathing with your movements.

8. Complete several repetitions, focusing on the fluidity of each movement.

You now have 12 methods to manage anxiety, and thus prevent it from sabotaging your efforts. Keep in mind that effective management during the test is also crucial. The next segment will cover how to handle it effectively.

Effective Management During the Test

To manage your performance and save time effectively, you must take into account a series of tricks. Rehearse them in advance so they become second nature on test day:

Divide the Time Available by the Number of Questions

Keep in mind the total time allocated for each section. For example, if you have 60 minutes for 60 questions, you have one minute for each, but some will be quicker to answer than others.

Answer the easiest and quickest questions to have more time for the difficult ones. If a question takes more than a minute, make an educated guess and move on. Return to the difficult ones if you have time left.

Read Quickly Before Starting

Do a quick scan to identify the easiest ones and those that might require more time. Focus on keywords and options. Don't try to understand every detail at this stage; instead, look for familiar topics and terms you can answer confidently.

During your practice sessions, work on understanding the general idea without going too deep. When you have read them all, decide which one to answer first.

This improves efficiency and reduces stress since you know what to expect and how to approach each section.

Use Elimination to Discard Incorrect Answers

Elimination is effective for improving your chances of selecting the correct answer. Review each option and eliminate those that are visibly incorrect, reducing the number of options and increasing your chances of getting it right.

Read each option carefully and identify any logical errors. For example, if a mathematics question asks you to add two numbers and one option is a negative number, eliminate it immediately.

By discarding the incorrect options, you reduce complexity and focus on the remaining options. This requires less effort and time, keeping you at a constant pace and avoiding getting stuck, which improves your ability to manage time and accuracy.

If One Takes More Than a Minute, Make an Educated Guess and Move On

I mentioned this to you in the first recommendation, now I'm going to explain how to do it: Read the options carefully and look for any clues guiding you to eliminate incorrect options. If you can rule out one or two options, your chances of choosing the right one increase.

An educated guess is based on the knowledge you already have. Even if you are not sure of the exact answer, use your intuition and the clues available to make the best possible choice.

This reduces pressure and stress. Train this skill in your practice tests, and you will feel more comfortable and confident during the real exam.

Use the Clock to Make Sure You are Moving Forward as Planned

This ensures you progress as planned and don't fall behind. Use a wristwatch or the clock provided in the room to monitor your progress.

Note the time and calculate how far you should be at certain scores before you begin. If you have 60 minutes for a 60-question section, check the clock every 15 minutes to verify you are completing approximately 15 questions in that interval.

Practice this during your sessions, use a timer to simulate real conditions, and adjust your pace accordingly.

Spend the Last Five Minutes Reviewing

During these final minutes, focus on verifying all questions are answered and you have not left any blank. This helps you detect mistakes you may have overlooked at the beginning due to the pressure.

Review questions that initially seemed difficult and verify your educated guesses make sense. If you have doubts about any of them, this is the time to reconsider and make changes if necessary. It is an opportunity to correct mistakes and ensure each answer is marked in the proper place.

Practice With Timed Mock Tests

Simulating test conditions allows you to get used to the pressure and structure of the real exam. This improves your mental stamina and assists you in knowing where to improve your efficiency.

It helps you develop the ability to concentrate for long periods.

Strategies for Guessing and Reviewing Work

You might think it is not a good idea to leave the results in the hands of "riddles," but it is not about guessing at random. It involves implementing strategies to make it easier to rule out and decide, I present them to you below:

Look for Common Patterns in Options

Sometimes correct answers on standardized tests follow certain patterns, so if you notice an option appearing repeatedly, it could be a clue. Pay attention to how they are presented. If three options are very similar and one is different, the different one is likely incorrect, use your prior knowledge and logic, and do not rely exclusively on this; combine it with other methods of elimination to improve your guesses

Consider the Length of the Answers

More detailed and specific options are more likely to be correct, so when reviewing them, pay attention to those longer. These options incorporate nuances indicating a deeper understanding of the material. However, don't automatically assume the longest is always correct.

To identify when an option might be correct, compare the information each gives. More detailed answers typically avoid absolute terms like "always" or "never" and instead use moderate terms like "often" or "usually." But don't choose one just because it's long; verify at all times it is relevant and accurate.

This way, you can filter options that seem incomplete or too general. Practice it in your mocks to become familiar with identification, thereby improving your ability to review and respond effectively during the ACT.

Check Consistency, Ensuring There Are No Contradictions

In the mathematics section, check that all your answers are consistent with the formulas and concepts you have used. If one asks you to calculate a distance and another asks you to calculate the time of a trip to that distance with a given speed, verify they are logical with each other. If you find inconsistencies, review them carefully to correct them.

In English, pay attention to the rules of grammar and style. If you have decided to use a particular structure, make sure the same structure applies to all related ones. If you choose an option using the active voice in a sentence, check other options that must be consistent using the active voice.

In the reading part, ensure the answers are consistent with the information provided.

Use Cross Feedback

Use what one question tells you to answer another. In the math section, if one item gives you a specific formula or value, take advantage of it to solve another problem. If you calculate the value of X in one and the next requires the value of X, use that result to simplify your work.

In English, pay attention to those asking for grammatical or stylistic corrections. If one teaches you a grammatical rule you didn't know, apply that rule to other similar ones. This improves your accuracy as you would be able to apply the newly acquired knowledge efficiently.

In reading, they usually refer to the same part of the passage. If one helps you understand better, use it to answer subsequent questions about it.

Keys to a Growth Mindset

To end this chapter, I have decided to present a series of keys that will help you stay in tune with your objectives and move forward without anything stopping you from reaching the goal you have set for yourself:

Accept Mistakes as Opportunities

Instead of feeling frustrated or unmotivated, try to see them as valuable lessons that bring you closer to success. Every time you make one, analyze what went wrong and what you could do differently next time. It allows you to discover your weaknesses and work on them constructively.

To develop it, try keeping a journal. After each session, write down the mistakes you made and reflect on them, asking yourself what caused them and how you could avoid them in the future.

This approach will allow you to better manage pressure and stress and remind yourself every challenge is an opportunity to improve. Staying calm will, in turn, improve your performance. Practice this in your daily studies, ensuring each mistake is a stone on the path to success.

Believe in Continuous Improvement Through Effort

Believing in continuous improvement through effort is essential to a growth mindset. This belief is based on the idea your skills and knowledge are developed through dedication and hard work. By internalizing this, you realize natural talent plays a part in success but constant and directed effort makes the difference.

To cultivate this belief, set goals that are challenging but achievable. Work on your weaknesses and celebrate every small progress you make. This reinforces the idea that what you are doing is paying off and motivates you to keep going. Practice self-praise by recognizing your progress.

During ACT prep, you will be able to persevere even when the material is difficult or when you face setbacks. You will not feel discouraged by a low score; instead, you will see each session and each test as an opportunity to improve.

Face Challenges as Opportunities to Grow

You will face several challenges, which you already know because I have mentioned some of them throughout this guide. They could be difficult questions that make you doubt your abilities, moments of stress overwhelming you, or topics you don't fully master. In these cases, tackle them head-on. Research more, look for different resources, and practice until you feel more confident. Every time you overcome a difficult topic, you are building your confidence because your understanding of the material improves.

Maintain a Positive and Resilient Attitude in the Face of Difficulties

Resilience is the ability to recover quickly from difficulties, while a positive attitude is characterized by hope in your abilities. Both qualities allow you to manage stress effectively.

Instead of thinking, "I'm not good at math," think, "I can get better at math with effort."

Resilience is developed through experience, so focus on the goals you have already formulated and move forward despite any setbacks. Implement each strategy I have shared to control anxiety, and you will be strengthening the resilience muscle.

Develop Self-Compassion and Patience Skills

This involves treating yourself with the same kindness and understanding you would offer a friend amid difficulty, accepting your mistakes and challenges without judging yourself harshly, being patient, and practicing perseverance in the face of obstacles.

Start with self-awareness, and observe your thoughts and emotions, especially when you make mistakes or feel overwhelmed. Instead of criticizing yourself, practice speaking kindly to yourself. Everyone faces difficulties. If you get a low score on a test, don't tell yourself things like "I'm terrible at this;" instead, you could say, "It's normal to have difficulties. What should I learn from this to improve?"

Accept progress may be slow and every small step is valuable. Set realistic expectations and celebrate every achievement, no matter how small.

Part II:
In-Depth Review and Practice by Section

Chapter 4: English Proficiency

In this chapter I will present all the aspects you must understand about grammar, punctuation, sentence structure, and rhetorical skills, to master English and be successful.

You will find all the theoretical content followed by a section of exercises, including mini-tests, to help you prepare for the ACT:

Grammar and Usage Fundamentals

Below are the basics to understand grammar:

Subject and Verb Agreement

This knowledge is vital to constructing correct sentences. To do this, the verb must coincide in number with the subject. If the verb is singular, it must also be singular; if the subject is plural, the verb must be plural.

To illustrate: in the sentence "She walks to school," "she" is singular, so "walks" is also singular.

Verb Tenses (Present, Past, Future)

They indicate when the action occurs. The present tense is used for habitual actions or general truths, such as "She studies every day." The past tense is used for actions that occurred at a specific time in the past, as in "She studied yesterday." The future refers to actions that will occur, such as "She will study tomorrow."

Avoid confusion: "She studies yesterday" is wrong because "yesterday" requires the past. The correct form is "She studied yesterday." Don't mix tenses without a clear reason. In "She studies every day and will study tomorrow," the tenses are used correctly because they describe actions at different times.

Verb Forms (Simple, Progressive, Perfect, Perfect Progressive)

These add nuances about the duration and status of the action. The simple form describes habitual or general actions: "She walks to school." The progressive form indicates actions in progress, such as "She is walking to school." The perfect form shows actions completed at another time, such as "She has walked to school." The perfect progressive form combines both aspects, indicating continuous actions that were completed, such as "She has been walking to school for an hour."

Pronouns (Personal, Possessive, Reflexive, Relative, Interrogative, Indefinite)

Pronouns replace nouns to avoid repetitions. Personal ones like "he," "she," and "it" refer to specific people or things. Possessives like "his," "her," and "their" indicate possession. Reflexives like "myself," and "yourself" reflect the action back to the subject, as in "She taught herself." Relatives like "who," "which," and "that" connect clauses, as in "The book that she read was interesting." Interrogatives like "who," "whom," and "whose" are used in questions, like "Whose book is this?" Indefinites like "someone," "anyone," and "everything" refer to non-specific people or things.

Always verify that the pronoun agrees in number and gender with the noun it replaces. In "Each student must bring their book," although "student" is singular, "their" is used to avoid specifying gender. Don't use reflexives incorrectly, as in "She taught to herself," which should be "She taught herself."

Adjectives and Adverbs

Adjectives describe nouns, as in "The quick fox," while adverbs modify verbs, adjectives, or other adverbs, as in "She runs quickly."

Don't use adjectives instead of adverbs, and vice versa. "He is a good singer" is appropriate because "good" describes the noun "singer." But "He sings well" is okay because "well" describes how he sings.

When comparing, use "er" for one-syllable adjectives and adverbs, and "more" for those with two or more syllables, such as "happier" and "more beautiful." In superlatives, use "est" or "most," as in "happiest" and "most beautiful."

Comparative and Superlative

They are used to compare things or people. Comparatives are used to compare two elements. For one-syllable adjectives, add "er" to the end of the adjective, as in "taller." For adjectives with two or more syllables, use "more" before the adjective, as in "more beautiful." Superlatives are used to compare three or more elements. For one-syllable adjectives, add "est" to the end of the adjective, as in "tallest." For adjectives with two or more syllables, use "most" before the adjective, as in "most beautiful."

Do not mix these formats. "She is more taller than her sister" is wrong. It should be "She is taller than her sister." And don't use double comparatives like "more better." The correct form is "better." For superlatives, don't use "most" with one-syllable adjectives. Instead of "most tall," use "tallest."

Conjunctions (Coordinates, Subordinates, Correlatives)

Conjunctions join words, phrases, or clauses. Coordinating conjunctions join elements of equal importance, such as "and," "but," and "or", such as: "She likes apples and oranges."

Subordinating conjunctions join a dependent clause to an independent one, such as "because," "although," and "if." An example is "She went to the park because it was sunny."

Correlative conjunctions work in pairs, such as "either...or," "neither...nor," "both...and," as in: "Neither the teacher nor the students knew the answer."

Be careful not to make the mistake of lack of agreement between the connected parts. In "Either the teachers or the principal are responsible," instead of "are," the correct form would be "is" to agree with "principal."

Prepositions and Prepositional Phrases

Prepositions indicate relationships of place, time, or direction, such as: "in," "on," "at," and "by." A prepositional phrase includes a preposition and its object, such as "on the table" or "by the river." These phrases add more details, describing where, when, or how something happens: "The book is on the table" and "She arrived at noon."

Proper Use of Idiomatic Phrases

They are expressions whose meaning cannot be deduced from the literal meaning of their words. As an example, "kick the bucket" means "to die," not "to kick a bucket".

To use them well, you must understand their meaning as well as their appropriate context. "Spill the beans" means "to reveal a secret" and is used in informal situations.

Elimination of Redundancies and Prolixity

Redundancy occurs when information is repeated unnecessarily: "He returned back to the house" is redundant because "returned" already implies "back." The correct form would be "He returned to the house."

Conciseness involves eliminating unnecessary words so that the writing is direct and clear. Instead of "In order to succeed, you must work hard," you could say "To succeed, you must work hard."

Precision in Language Use and Word Choice

Always choose the right words to express your ideas, "affect" and "effect" have different meanings and should be used appropriately: "The weather can affect your mood" and "The effect of the weather on your mood is noticeable."

Do not use complicated or far-fetched words; it is better to use clear and direct language that is easy to understand. Review your writing to verify that each word chosen conveys what you want to say.

Correct Use of Gerunds and Infinitives

Gerunds are verb forms that end in "ing" and function as nouns, as in "Swimming is fun."

Infinitives are the base form of the verb preceded by "to," as in "to swim." The use depends on the context. For example, "I enjoy swimming" is correct because "enjoy" is followed by a gerund. On the other hand, "I want to swim" is correct because "want" follows from an infinitive.

Be careful not to use the gerund or infinitive incorrectly after certain verbs. "She decided swimming" is not appropriate; it should be "She decided to swim." Likewise, "He is interested to learn" is wrong; it should be "He is interested in learning."

Correction of Ambiguities

This ensures your writing is clear and precise. An ambiguity occurs when a phrase is interpreted in more than one way. "She saw the man with the telescope" could mean she used the telescope to see the man or the man had a telescope. To correct this, clarify as follows: "She saw the man who had the telescope" or "Using the telescope, she saw the man."

Ambiguities similarly arise from pronouns with confusing antecedents: "When Sarah met Emma, she was excited" is ambiguous because it is not clear who was excited. Rewriting it as "When Sarah met Emma, Sarah was excited" removes the ambiguity.

Always proofread your writing to ensure every pronoun and phrase refers to its antecedents, eliminating any potential confusion for the reader.

Appropriate Style and Tone

Style refers to the way the text is structured and presented, while tone reflects the writer's attitude toward the topic and the reader.

For the ACT, you need to adjust both based on context; a persuasive essay should have a convincing and confident tone, while a descriptive essay might be more detailed and evocative.

Phrases like "gonna" or "wanna" are inappropriate in an academic essay. Instead, use "going to" or "want to."

Relative Pronouns and Their Correct Use (Who, Whom, Whose, Which, That)

These connect clauses and give additional information about a noun.

- "Who" is used for subjects: "The student who studies hard will succeed."
- "Whom" is used for objects: "The teacher whom you met is my favorite."
- "Whose" indicates possession: "The artist whose work you admire is here."
- "Which" is used for things: "The book, which is on the table, is mine."
- "That" is used for people and things in essential clauses: "The car that I bought is red."

Be careful not to use "who" for "whom."

Differentiation Between Homophones (There, Their, They're; Your, You're; Its, It's)

Understanding this difference will allow you to have good grammar. In this sense "There" refers to a place, as in "The book is over there." "Their" is possessive, indicating belonging, as in "Their house is big." "They're" is a contraction of "they are," as in "They're going to the park."

For "your" and "you're," "your" is possessive, as in "Is this your pen?" "You're" is the contraction of "you are," as in "You're my best friend."

In the case of "its" and "it's" they could be confusing. "Its" is possessive, as in "The cat licked its paw." "It's" is a contraction of "it is" or "it has," as in "It's raining" or "It's been a long day."

To use homophones ideally, you could pronounce the word with "they are," "you are," or "it is." If it still makes sense, use the corresponding contraction. In "It's a nice day," replacing "it's" with "it is" works, confirming the contraction is correct.

Punctuation and Sentence Structure

Below, divided into two parts, I present these significant aspects for your preparation:

Punctuation

Commas

They are used to separate elements in a series, as in "I bought apples, oranges, and bananas." Likewise, to separate independent clauses joined by conjunctions such as "and," "but," and "or," as in: "She wanted to go to the park, but it started raining." You could use them after introductions, as in "After the movie, we went to dinner. However, avoid both excessive and insufficient use of commas.

Semicolons

They connect independent clauses that are related, as in "I have a big exam tomorrow; I can't go out tonight." They are used to separate items in a list that already contains commas: "The meeting was attended by John, the manager; Mary, the assistant; and Tom, the intern."

You should not use them to connect a dependent clause to an independent one. Instead of: "Although it was raining; we went out," the appropriate thing would be: "Although it was raining, we went out."

Colons

They are used to introduce a list, an explanation, or a quote, as in: "She bought three things: apples, oranges, and bananas." Colons are used to emphasize a conclusion or explanation, as in "He had only one hobby: reading. "

Don't use them after a clause that directly introduces a list, as in "Her hobbies include: reading, writing, and swimming." Instead, write "Her hobbies include reading, writing, and swimming."

Hyphens

They connect words in compounds like "well-known" or "long-term"; they are also used to break up words at the end of a line if they don't fit in full.

Avoid errors like: "He is a well known author" should be "He is a well-known author." Don't use hyphens for non-compound words, like "highschool," which should be "high school."

Parenthesis

They are used to insert additional information or clarifications within a sentence without interrupting the main flow: "She finally answered (after taking five minutes to think) she did not understand the question."

Quotation marks

They are used to frame direct quotes, as in "He said, 'I'll be there at six.'" Also for indicating titles of articles, book chapters, and words or phrases that are mentioned.

Punctuation should be placed inside the quotes. For example, "Did she really say 'amazing'?" is correct.

Apostrophes

They indicate possession and contractions. For possession, add an apostrophe followed by an "s" for singular nouns, such as "the cat's toy." For plural nouns ending in "s," just add an apostrophe, like "the cats' toys." In contractions, they replace omitted letters, as in "don't" (do not) and "it's" (it is or it has). Do not use apostrophes for plurals, as in "apple's," which should be "apples."

Sentence Structure

Parts of the sentence

You need a subject, a verb, and usually an object. First, identify the person, place, or idea acting, as in "The dog." The verb describes the action or state, as in "barks." The object receives the action, as in "The dog barks at the mailman."

Structure of simple, compound, complex, and compound-complex sentences

Simple sentences have a subject and a verb, as in "She runs." They are clear and direct, while compound clauses combine two independent clauses with a conjunction, as in "She runs, and he walks."

Complex clauses have one independent clause and at least one dependent clause, as in "She runs because she enjoys it."

Compound-complex sentences combine both structures, as in "She runs because she enjoys it, and he walks because he needs exercise."

Run-ons and how to correct them (fused sentences and comma splices)

Run-ons occur when two or more independent clauses are combined without the proper conjunction. Fused sentences are a type where they are joined without punctuation, as in "She loves to read she goes to the library often." To correct this, you could do it like this: "She loves to read. She goes to the library often." Another option is to use a conjunction: "She loves to read, so she goes to the library often."

Comma splices are another type of run-on where commas are used incorrectly to join independent clauses, as in "She loves to read, she goes to the library often." To correct a comma splice, use a semicolon: "She loves to read; she goes to the library often." Or you could add a conjunction: "She loves to read, and she goes to the library often."

Modifiers and their proper placement

Modifiers should be placed close to the words they modify to avoid confusion; a misplaced one is an adjective, adverb, or phrase not connected to the word it modifies, which changes the meaning, as in: "She drove almost her kids to school every day" which suggests she didn't do it every day, but came close to doing it. The correct form is "She drove her kids to school almost every day."

Dangling modifiers do not have a clear word to modify. "Walking down the street, the trees were beautiful" suggests the trees were walking. The correction would be: "Walking down the street, she found the trees were beautiful."

Structure and function of independent and dependent clauses

Independent sentences are complete sentences that can stand alone, as in "She went to the store." They have a subject and a verb that form a complete idea. Dependent clauses cannot be alone and need an independent one to give complete meaning. "Because she was hungry" is a dependent clause that needs an independent one, as in "She went to the store because she was hungry."

Active and passive voice

In the active voice, the subject performs the action of the verb, as in "The cat chased the mouse." This structure is direct and clear. In the passive, the subject receives the action of the verb, as in "The mouse was chased by the cat."

The active voice is preferable because it is more concise and energetic. "The chef cooked the meal" is more direct than "The meal was cooked by the chef."

The passive voice is useful when you want to emphasize the action instead of the subject, or when the subject is unknown, as in "The letters were sent."

Grammatical parallelism

It is based on using the same grammatical structure in different parts to improve clarity and flow. As in "She likes running, swimming, and biking," which is correct because all activities use the same verb form "-ing." On the other hand, "She likes running, to swim, and biking" is not due to the inconsistency in the structure.

An example would be: "He is not only a great singer but also a skilled dancer," where both elements of the comparison maintain the same structure.

Rhetorical Skills

Rhetorical skills cover a large percentage of this part of the test, so keep the following points in mind:

Identify the Purpose

For this, you must understand the intention; it could be trying to inform, persuade, entertain, or explain something. Observe the tone: if it is neutral and presents facts, the purpose could be to inform. Another key aspect is the structure. If background is provided, a problem is presented, and solutions are suggested, the text is trying to persuade.

Understand the Audience

It involves determining who it was written for and adapting your analysis accordingly. The audience influences the tone, style, and content. An academic article uses formal language and technical terms because it is addressed to experts or students in that field. On the other hand, a travel blog uses a more casual and accessible tone because its audience is more general. Look for clues like vocabulary and cultural references. If terms specific to an industry or field are mentioned, the writer is targeting professionals. Taking into account the medium in which it is published, an article in a scientific journal has a different target audience than a publication in an entertainment magazine.

Distinguish Between Tone and Style

Tone refers to the attitude towards the topic or the reader; it could be formal, informal, sarcastic, serious, or optimistic, among others. To determine if it has a humorous tone, identify if there are jokes and light-hearted language, while an academic essay would have a more serious and formal tone. Style, on the other hand, is the specific way language is used to communicate the message. It includes aspects such as word choice, sentence structure, and figures of speech. A descriptive and detailed style is characterized by containing many metaphors and adjectives, and a direct and concise style has short and clear sentences.

Analyze the Structure of the Argument

It consists of breaking down how ideas are presented to persuade the reader. To do this you must discover what the argument is, which is usually found at the beginning. Then, notice how supporting elements are organized. Are testimonials, examples, or case studies used? If well structured, it follows a logical flow, starting with a general statement, then providing specific evidence, and concluding with a reflection. Similarly, you should analyze counterarguments. Are potential objections anticipated and refuted effectively? Analyzing these elements allows you to evaluate robustness.

Evaluate the Effectiveness of the Evidence Presented

For this, you must analyze whether the type of evidence supports the argument: is it a statistic, an anecdote, a testimony, or a quote from an authority? If you say "70% improved grades after implementing the program," you are using statistics to back up your claim. Next, evaluate the relevance; ask yourself if it relates to the thesis and if it is sufficient. Take into account the credibility of the source; statistics from academic research have more weight than personal anecdotes. To strengthen the argument, see if it is used logically and clearly, and if it is well integrated and explained.

Persuasive Techniques

Some include the use of logic (logos), appealing to emotions (pathos), and establishing credibility (ethos). Another is the rhetoric of the question, where a question is posed whose answer is obvious, as in "Isn't it obvious that we need change?" This invites the reader to reflect and agree. There could be the use of repetition to emphasize a key idea or contrasts to highlight differences.

Rhetorical Strategies

They are used to persuade, inform, or entertain your readers. Irony and hyperbole are key examples. Irony occurs when the literal meaning of words is contrary to what is intended to be expressed, creating an effect of surprise or humor. For example: "How lucky I am to be stuck in traffic!" It conveys frustration, not joy. Hyperbole is an intentional exaggeration for emphasis, as in "I'm so tired I could sleep for a year." It highlights an idea by taking it to the extreme. Others include the use of metaphors and similes. A metaphor says that one thing is another, as in "Time is money," while a simile compares two things using "like" or "as," as in "Quick as lightning." To master them, watch how they play with meaning and emotion. Notice how they are used to influence the reader's perception and reinforce your message.

Distinguish Between Facts and Opinions

A fact is a verifiable statement, based on objective and concrete evidence. In this sense, "The Earth orbits the Sun" is a fact because it is scientifically verifiable. However, opinions are subjective statements based on personal beliefs, feelings, or judgments, such as "Chocolate is the best flavor of ice cream." To distinguish between them, look for clues in language. Words like "I believe," "I think," and "I feel" usually indicate an opinion; facts are usually specific and quantifiable.

Evaluate the Use of Examples and Analogies

An example illustrates something concrete by describing a specific situation; if you argue that "practice improves performance," you could talk about an athlete who improves his performance with constant training. Analogies compare two different things that have something in common to help understand a complex concept. "Human memory works like a filing cabinet" is an analogy that helps visualize how we store and retrieve information. To evaluate the use of these two resources, you must analyze whether they serve to clarify. Are they relevant and easy to understand? Do they provide credibility?

Biases and Prejudices

A bias is an inclination or preference influencing objectivity; a political article written by an author affiliated with a specific political party could show a bias in favor of that party's policies and against those of the opposing party. To identify biases, look for loaded language, words, or phrases with strong emotional connotations, and pay attention to the selection of facts. See if opposing ideas are presented fairly or dismissed without proper analysis. A prejudice is an opinion formed without sufficient knowledge, which could be conscious or unconscious. To find them, you must question the underlying assumptions and see if these are based on stereotypes or generalizations.

Practice Questions (Mini Tests)

Below is a series of questions designed to help you strengthen your skills:

Grammar Foundation and Usage

Concordance between subject and verb

1. She _____ (be) very intelligent.

2. The dogs _____ (bark) all night.

3. My brother and I _____ (play) soccer on the weekends.

4. The group _____ (be) very excited about the concert.

5. Each of the students _____ (have) their book.

Verb tenses (present, past, future)

1. She _____ (run) every day.

2. Last year, they _____ (travel) to Europe.

3. Tomorrow, I _____ (study) for the exam.

4. We _____ (eat) pizza last night.

5. He ____ (live) in London in the future.

Verb forms (simple, progressive, perfect, perfect progressive)

1. She ____ (talk) on the phone right now. (Present Progressive)

2. We ____ (finish) the project yesterday. (Simple Past)

3. They ____ (live) here for ten years. (Present Perfect)

4. I ____ (read) a book for two hours. (Present Perfect Progressive)

5. Tomorrow at this time, he ____ (travel) to Paris. (Future Progressive)

Pronouns (personal, possessive, reflexive, relative, interrogative, indefinite)

1. ____ (He/They) is my best friend.

2. That backpack is ____ (your/mine).

3. I see ____ (myself/yourself) in the mirror.

4. The person ____ (who/whom) called left a message.

5. ____ (Who/Which) of them is the fastest?

Adjectives and adverbs

1. The movie was ____ (good/better).

2. She runs very ____ (quick/quickly).

3. The dog is ____ (large/largely).

4. He spoke ____ (soft/softly).

5. The book is ____ (interesting/interestingly).

Comparative and superlative

1. She is ____ (taller/the tallest) than her sister.

2. This is the ____ (best/better) book ever.

3. My car is ____ (faster/the fastest) than yours.

4. Everest is the ____ (higher/highest) mountain in the world.

5. This problem is the____ (less difficult/least difficult) to solve.

Conjunctions (coordinates, subordinates, correlatives)

1. Not only he is intelligent ____ (and/but) he is also very kind.

2. ____ (Although/But) he didn't have money, he went to the movies.

3. Neither you _____ (nor/and) I know the answer.

4. _____ (Because/But) he was tired, he decided to stay home.

5. Choose between studying now _____ (or/and) studying later.

Prepositions and prepositional phrases

1. The cat is _____ (on/at) the table.

2. She comes _____ (from/with) the store.

3. The book is _____ (between/on) the bed.

4. We will meet _____ (in/in front) of the school.

5. I'm tired _____ (because/because of) work.

Proper use of idiomatic phrases

1. Being in the clouds means _____ (being distracted/being on a plane).

2. To screw up means _____ (to make a mistake/to put something in your foot).

3. In fact, breast means _____ (accept the consequences/repair something).

4. Being dusted means _____ (to be tired/to be dust).

5. Having the upper hand means _____ (being in control/having mastery).

Elimination of redundancies and prolixity

1. She climbed up the mountain. (Identify and eliminate redundancy)

2. It is necessary that you arrive on time. (Rewrite more concisely)

3. Repeat what you said again. (Eliminate redundancy)

4. The fact that it is Monday means that it is the first day of the week. (Rewrite more concisely)

5. In my personal opinion, I think we should start now. (Eliminate redundancy)

Precision in language use and word choice

1. The report was _____ (good/interesting).

2. We need a clear _____ (strategy/tactics).

3. The president _____ (announced/stated) his decision.

4. She has a _____ (great/strong) personality.

5. The meeting was _____ (long/tedious).

Correct use of gerunds and infinitives

1. She enjoys ____ (read/reading) books at night.

2. It is important to ____ (do/doing) exercise frequently.

3. He is interested in ____ (learn/learning) new skills.

4. Before ____ (leave/leaving), make sure you turn off the lights.

5. I prefer to ____ (walk/walking) to work instead of driving.

Correction of ambiguities

1. I saw the man with the binoculars. (Rewrite to remove ambiguity)

2. The neighbor's dog that barks a lot is annoying. (Rewrite to remove ambiguity)

3. She said she would call her mother when she arrived. (Rewrite to remove ambiguity)

4. I brought my book and Carlos's notebook. (Rewrite to remove ambiguity)

5. Juan saw María when leaving the store. (Rewrite to remove ambiguity)

Appropriate style and tone

1. Write a formal letter requesting information about a university.

2. Compose an informal email to a friend about your weekend plans.

3. Write a persuasive speech about the relevance of recycling.

4. Write a descriptive essay about your favorite place.

5. Write a critical review of a book you have read.

Relative pronouns and their correct use (who, whom, whose, which, that)

1. The person ____ (who/whom) called me was my uncle.

2. The book ____ (who/that) I bought is very interesting.

3. The girl ____ (whose/who) dog was lost was crying.

4. The team ____ (who/that) won the match was very happy.

5. Do you know ____ (who/whom) to call for more information?

Differentiation between homophones (there, their, they're; your, you're; its, it's)

1. ____ (There/Their/They're) going to the park.

2. _____ **(Your/You're)** book is on the table.

3. The cat licked _____ **(its/it's)** paw.

4. _____ **(Their/They're/There)** house is beautiful.

5. Do you know _____ **(your/you're)** schedule for tomorrow?

Punctuation

Punctuation

1. Add the necessary punctuation: "She said she would come but she never showed up."

2. Point out and correct the punctuation error: "The book, which I read, is very interesting."

3. Where should punctuation marks go? "Pedro asked me if I would come tomorrow."

4. Rewrite using the correct punctuation: "Although it is early he is already awake."

Commas

1. Place the commas where they apply: "If you come in the morning we can go for a walk."

2. Rewrite using commas: "My sister who lives in Paris is coming to visit."

3. Where is a comma missing? "We need bread, milk and eggs."

4. Add commas to separate the clauses: "Before you leave make sure you close the door."

Semicolons

1. Put where it belongs: "I'm tired I've worked all day."

2. Rewrite using a semicolon: "Yesterday we went to the movies we saw an action movie."

3. How do you correct it with a semicolon? "I didn't go to the party I was sick."

4. Add the semicolon to connect two related ideas: "I like chocolate I prefer vanilla ice cream."

Colons

1. Place colons where they correspond: "We need the following ingredients flour, sugar, and eggs."

2. Rewrite using a colon: "There is something I can't stand dishonesty."

3. Where should the colon go? "She had a quality that everyone admired her generosity."

4. Add the colon to introduce a list: "In my backpack I carry three things books, a notebook, and a pen."

Hyphens

1. Hyphen where appropriate: "She is a very dedicated second year student."

2. Rewrite using hyphens: "It is a decision that we must make at the management level."

3. Where is a hyphen missing? "The project is in a pre production phase."

4. Add the hyphens to clarify the following compound: "She gave me a well known book about self-care."

Parenthesis

1. Place parentheses where appropriate: "The president of the John Doe company will make an announcement tomorrow."

2. Rewrite using parentheses: "My sister who lives in London is coming for Christmas."

3. Where are the parentheses missing? "The author of the novel which won the award is very well known."

4. Add parentheses to include additional information: "The conference will be on March 15th and 16th."

Quotation Marks

1. Place quotation marks where appropriate: "She said I'm not going to the party."

2. Rewrite using quotation marks correctly: "The poem begins with the line In a place in La Mancha."

3. Where are the quotation marks missing? "He asked me, what do you want to do tomorrow."

4. Add quotation marks to indicate a title: "The book Pride and Prejudice is a classic."

Apostrophes

1. Place the apostrophe where appropriate: "Johns car is in the garage."

2. Rewrite using apostrophes correctly: "Annas apples are very delicious."

3. Where is the apostrophe missing? "It's the managers responsibility."

4. Add apostrophes to indicate possession: "The book of Peter is on the table."

Sentence Structure

Parts of the sentence

1. Point out the subject, verb, and object: "Mary bought a book."

2. Write one sentence where the subject is "The cat" and the verb is "sleep."

3. Rewrite to include an indirect object: "John sent a letter."

4. Identify the parts: "The teacher explained the lesson to the students."

Structure of simple, compound, complex, and compound-complex sentences

1. Combine these two sentences to form a compound one: "Pedro plays soccer. Ana studies."

2. Transform into a compound-complex sentence: "The teacher explained the lesson, and the students took notes, although some were distracted."

3. Explain the difference between a simple sentence and a compound one.

Run-ons and how to correct them (fused sentences and comma splices)

1. Correct the fused sentence: "Maria is very intelligent she always gets good grades."

2. Identify and correct the comma splice: "He went to the park, she went to the store."

3. Rewrite to remove the run-on: "They arrived early they sat in the front row."

4. Explain how to avoid run-ons in writing.

Modifiers and their proper placement

1. What is the misplaced modifier: "I almost see all the students finish the exam."

2. Correct misplaced modifier: "She only has two cats."

3. Rewrite the sentence with the modifier placed: "He almost drives his car every day."

4. Where should the modifier go? "Juan's car new is red."

Structure and function of independent and dependent clauses

1. What is the independent clause: "Even though he was tired, he continued working."

2. Rewrite to include an independent clause: "When he got home, he had dinner."

3. Explain the difference between an independent clause and a dependent clause.

Active and passive voice

1. Rewrite in passive voice: "The dog chased the cat."

2. Change to active voice: "The letter was written by María."

3. Explain when it is more effective to use the active voice instead of the passive.

Grammatical parallelism

1. What is the parallelism error: "He likes to swim, running and cycling."

2. Correct to maintain parallelism: "He prefers reading books and watch movies."

3. What is parallelism and why is it important in writing?

4. Rewrite to achieve parallelism: "She wants to travel to Europe, learn French, and making new friends."

Rhetorical Skills

Identify the purpose

1. What is the purpose of an author writing about the relevance of environmental conservation in the following paragraph? "Environmental conservation preserves biodiversity, and secures natural resources for future generations."

2. What purpose could an essay discussing the effects of climate change serve?

3. Explain how you would state an author's purpose in an academic essay.

Understand the audience

1. What characteristics would the audience of an article on technology for seniors have? Excerpt: "Technological innovations in mobile devices have improved the quality of life of older people, allowing them to stay connected with their loved ones and access health services more easily."

2. How would you adapt a nutrition message for an audience of athletes? Excerpt: "A balanced diet is essential for maintaining optimal performance and rapid recovery after intense workouts."

3. Explain why it is important to know your audience when writing a speech.

Distinguish between tone and style

1. Describe the tone: "I am pleased to announce that we have exceeded our sales expectations this quarter, thanks to the dedicated efforts of our team."

2. What is the style of the following excerpt and how does it differ in tone? "The sun was slowly setting on the horizon, turning the sky a warm orange that was reflected in the calm waters of the lake."

3. Analyze the tone of the following sentence: "I'm excited about the project we're about to start."

Analyze the structure of the argument

1. State the main premise: "Regular exercise improves physical health, and has a positive impact on mental health, reducing stress and anxiety levels."

2. How would you identify the structure of an argument in the following fragment? "To combat climate change, it is crucial to reduce carbon emissions. This is possible through the use of renewable energy and the implementation of stricter environmental policies."

3. Explain the relevance of a clear structure in a persuasive argument.

4. Rewrite an argument about the need to recycle to make it more coherent and persuasive.

Evaluate the effectiveness of the evidence presented

1. What makes the evidence in the following excerpt compelling? "A recent study shows that 70% of people who practice yoga report a significant decrease in stress levels."

2. How would you evaluate the relevance of the evidence in the following excerpt? "Countries that have implemented renewable energy policies have seen a 30% reduction in carbon emissions in the last five years."

3. Explain the difference between anecdotal and statistical evidence and give an example of each.

Persuasive techniques

1. Determine the persuasive technique: "Don't be left behind, buy now and join thousands of satisfied people."

2. Which technique is used in the following sentence? "Our clients have experienced visible improvements in just one week."

3. Explain how persuasive techniques influence the audience.

4. Rewrite using a different persuasive technique: "This product has been tested to deliver exceptional results."

Rhetorical strategies

1. Identify the rhetorical strategy: "The sunlight caressed the leaves of the trees."

2. What rhetorical strategy is used in the following fragment? "Time is a thief that never gives back what it takes."

3. Explain how rhetorical strategies improve a text.

4. Rewrite to include a different rhetorical strategy: "His words were like arrows, direct and accurate."

Distinguish between facts and opinions

1. Is this a fact or an opinion? "Chocolate is the best sweet in the world."

2. Identify the opinion: "I think cats are more affectionate than dogs."

3. Explain why it is important to distinguish between facts and opinions in an argument.

4. Rewrite to make it an opinion instead of a fact: "Everest is the highest mountain in the world."

Evaluate the use of examples and analogies

1. Is the use of examples in the following fragment effective? "Just like a plant needs water, children need love to grow."

2. Analyze how the example is used: "Just as a seed needs fertile soil to grow, students need a suitable environment."

3. Explain the relevance of using examples and analogies in writing.

Biases and Prejudices

1. Point out the bias: "Only students from the best universities can succeed."

2. Is there any bias in the following fragment? "All teenagers are irresponsible."

3. Explain why it is important to recognize biases in writing.

Now, you are ready to move on to the next chapter.

Chapter 5: Reading Comprehension

The Reading section is crucial to master, requiring strong comprehension skills. Therefore, strategies for preparation and exam day implementation are essential.

You will find similarities in the skills needed for English comprehension because mastering grammar is crucial to effectively understanding and mastering various passages.

So read very carefully, but importantly, do the exercises and questions included at the end:

Critical Reading and Annotation Techniques for the ACT Test

Start by learning and becoming an expert in these techniques:

Skimming

With this, it is possible to grasp the general idea without stopping excessively. For this skill, read long articles and focus on the first and last sentences of each paragraph, paying attention to headings, subheadings, and bold or italicized words. During the ACT, use skimming to get an overview, don't dwell on words you don't immediately understand. The goal is to get a quick, general understanding of the content; it will help you know which sections will need deeper reading.

Scanning

With this, instead of grasping a general idea, you focus on searching for specific content. Read long texts and select keywords. Scan with your eyes without reading every word.

This way you can use it to find specific answers. The procedure will be simple because you only have to read the questions and mentally underline the keywords. Then, scan for those keywords or related ideas.

Find Context for Unknown Vocabulary

When you find a word that you don't understand, don't stop and look up its meaning in a dictionary. Instead, look at the words and sentences around it. Look at how the word is used in the sentence: is it a noun, verb, or adjective? What other words are associated with it? What images or ideas does it evoke?

This approach will improve your ability to interpret and understand new terms more quickly and maintain reading flow without unnecessary interruptions.

Mark the Transitions

Transitions are words or phrases that connect ideas or paragraphs. Words such as "however," "furthermore," "on the other hand," and "consequently" indicate changes of direction or additions.

Read articles and essays, paying special attention to transition words and phrases. By mentally marking them, you will be able to understand how ideas are structured better and it will allow you to follow the author's train of thought more effectively, which will be useful in answering questions about the structure and relationships between ideas.

Identify Rhetorical Questions

As mentioned earlier, rhetorical questions emphasize or prompt reflection without expecting an answer; recognizing these questions aids in understanding the author's intentions and tone. When encountering a rhetorical question, pause to consider its purpose and its relevance to the overall narrative.

All of this will help you interpret and understand the content in greater depth and respond more accurately.

Find Repetitive Patterns

Authors often repeat keywords, phrases, or ideas for emphasis and to make sure the reader gets the whole idea. Finding them helps you understand the main ideas and recurring themes.

Read texts from various genres and take note of words or phrases that are repeated. Ask yourself why you chose to emphasize these terms and how they contribute to understanding. As you read, keep an eye out for any repetition.

Mental Paraphrasing

To do this, you must rephrase what you just read using your own words, this way your understanding is reinforced.

To become an expert, choose an essay from an ACT preparation book, read a paragraph containing a main idea and several supporting details, and rephrase the main idea and what is most relevant.

Practice it with different types of texts: narrative, informative, and persuasive. In narrative texts paraphrase the main actions and motivations of the characters; in informative texts, focus on relevance; and in persuasive texts, reformulate the arguments and evidence presented.

During the ACT, use this technique after reading each paragraph. If one details the causes and effects of a historical event, paraphrase the main causes and their direct consequences.

Ask Questions While You Read

These force you to interact with the content and evaluate its relevance and coherence.

To implement it effectively, start by reading a passage on a specific topic, such as an essay on climate change. As you read, ask questions such as: "What is the author's position on climate change?", "What evidence is presented to support this position?", "How does it connect to what was discussed before?" and "What are the implications?" In an argumentative one, ask yourself: "What arguments does the author use to convince the reader?" and "How does the author refute possible objections?"

You could turn the titles and subtitles into questions. If the title is "Impact of deforestation on biodiversity," ask yourself: "How does deforestation impact biodiversity?" Then, look for the answers as you read.

Identify Inferences

This skill is necessary to understand the full meaning, as it usually requires you to make inferences based on what you have read.

To develop it, select a narrative fragment where a character's feelings or motivations are not directly stated. Read the passage and ask yourself what emotions the characters might be experiencing based on their actions and dialogue. Then, verify your deductions with the rest of the text or by consulting literary analysis.

When you are on the exam, if you describe a scene in nature and mention the stillness of the place and the gentle sounds of water, infer the environment is calm and relaxing, even if it is not said explicitly.

Another way to practice this technique is through group discussion and analysis. Read together with a friend or tutor and share the inferences each of you made. Discuss why you came to them and what clues you based them on.

Evaluate Consistency

This involves analyzing how ideas and arguments are connected and whether they flow in a logical and organized way. To do this, take an academic article or essay and divide it into paragraphs. Rearrange them and then try to put them back in the original order. This exercise forces you to understand how ideas are related and how one idea leads to the next. Use this method, especially when reading long passages. Pay attention to transition words and phrases such as "therefore," "however," and "in addition," which indicate the relationship between ideas. Evaluate whether it follows a logical development, beginning with a clear introduction, followed by well-developed supporting points, and ending with a coherent conclusion. In the days before the exam, use texts with very clearly defined structures, such as scientific articles and academic essays. Read them and analyze how each section contributes to the overall argument. Write your essays and ask others to evaluate them in terms of coherence. This feedback on how you connect your ideas and how they flow will help you develop a critical eye.

Identify Conclusions

These summarize the central idea the author wants to convey, based on the evidence presented.

You should look for statements that seem to bring together or synthesize; these are usually at the end of paragraphs, where you tie up loose ends and present a final idea.

Pay attention to transition words and phrases that introduce final ideas, such as "therefore," and "in short," which often precede them and distinguish them from the rest.

Take persuasive essays and underline the conclusions. Then, compare your selections with expert analysis or reference answers to see if you have identified the main idea. By doing this in your sessions, you will become an expert.

Distinguish Between Important Information and Minor Details

The important details are those that contribute to the central idea, while the minor details are additional elements that provide context but are not essential to overall understanding.

Practice with newspaper articles or book chapters. Read a paragraph, and underline the main ideas you think would be important for a summary. Then, review the minor details and ask yourself if you could leave them out without losing the overall meaning of the paragraph.

On the ACT, use selective reading. In each paragraph, focus on the first and last sentences, as they usually contain the main ideas. Quickly read the middle content to capture the details that support those main ideas.

During practice, try to outline. Place main ideas as headings and minor details as supporting points.

Strategies to Approach the Reading Section

With these, you can speed up:

Read the Questions Before the Passage

This allows you to discover the specific information you need as you read. It enables you to pay more attention to relevant details and minimize the minutes you spend on parts of the text that are not essential to answer.

Find Connections Between Paragraphs

This involves capturing transition words and phrases indicating how ideas are related between different sections.

By understanding these connections, you can follow the author's argument more clearly and respond accurately, making it easier to anticipate complex questions and improve your performance in the reading section.

Analyze the Argumentative Structure of the Text

To analyze it, look for the author's main statement, and see how it develops throughout the text. Notice how the author contrasts different criteria and refutes counterarguments.

To practice, analyze various texts and see how they connect. This skill will allow you to break down and understand the argument structure during the ACT.

Distinguish Between Comparisons and Contrasts

Distinguishing between comparisons and contrasts allows you to understand how similarities and differences between concepts are presented. To do this, look for words and phrases that indicate comparison, such as "similarly" or "likewise," and contrast, such as "in contrast" or "whereas."

Read carefully to find points that show how two or more items are similar or different.

Practice by selecting texts that use these techniques and underlining sections that indicate comparison or contrast.

Finalize Transitions Between Ideas

Look for words and phrases that connect one idea to another, such as "however," "therefore," "in addition," and "consequently." These transitions indicate logical relationships, such as contrast, cause and effect, or addition.

Observe how each transition guides the reader from one point to the next, giving coherence to the text.

Use Elimination for Incorrect Options in Questions

Read each answer choice and eliminate those that are irrelevant, contradictory, or do not align with the text. Review keywords and details to catch options that do not fit. This allows you to focus on the most likely options and improve accuracy in the reading section.

Practice Passages and Question Analysis

To help you develop skills, practice with these two compendiums:

Compendium 1

#1: History

In 1776, the Second Continental Congress of the United States approved the Declaration of Independence, marking the beginning of the fight for the independence of the American colonies from British rule. This document, written by Thomas Jefferson, proclaimed the equality of all men and their inalienable right to life, liberty, and the pursuit of happiness. Despite opposition and hardship, the settlers' perseverance culminated in the creation of a new nation based on democratic principles.

#1: What was the main function of the Declaration of Independence according to the passage?

- A) Establish a new government.

- B) Declare war against Great Britain.

- C) Proclaim equality and inalienable rights.

- D) End the War of Independence.

Analysis: The correct one is C. It underlines that the Declaration of Independence proclaimed the equality of all men and their right to life, liberty, and the pursuit of happiness.

2: Science

Stem cells have the unique ability to develop into many different types of cells in the body. In the initial stage of development, pluripotent stem cells differentiate into cells of the skin, heart, brain, and other organs. This potential makes them a valuable tool for regenerative medicine, as they are used to repair damaged tissues or treat degenerative diseases. However, the use of stem cells raises ethical and scientific questions that have yet to be resolved.

#2: According to the passage, why are pluripotent stem cells valuable?

- A) They can divide quickly.

- B) They can develop in many different types of cells.

- C) They do not raise ethical questions.

- D) They are easy to obtain.

Analysis: The correct one is B. It highlights that pluripotent stem cells differentiate into many different types of cells, making them valuable for regenerative medicine.

#3: Literature

In her novel "Wuthering Heights," Emily Brontë explores the complexity of human emotions through the characters of Heathcliff and Catherine. The work portrays a passionate but destructive love, set in the bleak moors of Yorkshire. The non-linear narrative and use of multiple perspectives offer unusual depth in characterization, allowing readers to understand each character's motives and internal struggles.

#3: What literary technique does Brontë use to offer unusual depth in characterization?

- A) Direct dialogue
- B) Detailed description
- C) Non-linear narrative and multiple perspectives
- D) Poetic language

Analysis: The correct one is C. It mentions that Brontë uses non-linear narrative and multiple perspectives to offer unusual depth in characterization.

4: Environment

Deforestation in the Amazon has reached alarming levels, with vast areas of forest cleared to make way for agriculture and livestock. This phenomenon destroys the habitat of countless species and contributes to climate change by releasing large amounts of carbon dioxide. Initiatives to curb deforestation include conservation policies, reforestation, and the promotion of sustainable agricultural practices.

#4: What is one of the effects of deforestation in the Amazon according to the passage?

- A) Improvement of agricultural production
- B) Increase in species in danger of extinction
- C) Contribution to climate change
- D) Expansion of urban areas

Analysis: The correct one is C. It mentions that deforestation contributes to climate change by releasing large amounts of carbon dioxide.

#5: Psychology

The placebo effect is a fascinating phenomenon in which a patient experiences an improvement in their condition after receiving an inert treatment because they believe they are receiving an effective intervention. Studies have shown positive expectation triggers a series of physiological responses, including the release of endorphins and other neurotransmitters that improve well-being.

#5: What triggers the placebo effect according to the passage?

- A) The treatment itself
- B) The patient's positive expectation
- C) The severity of the patient's condition
- D) The duration of treatment

Analysis: The correct one is B. It indicates that the patient's positive expectation triggers physiological responses improving well-being, highlighting the relevance of the mind-body connection.

#6: Economy

Globalization has transformed the world economy, facilitating international trade and capital mobility. However, it has generated significant inequalities, as the benefits of globalization are not distributed equally. While some regions thrive with new market opportunities, others struggle with job losses and environmental degradation. To mitigate these effects, it is essential to implement policies that promote sustainable development and economic equity.

#6: What is one of the negative consequences of globalization according to the passage?

- A) It facilitates international trade.
- B) Capital mobility increases.
- C) It generates significant inequalities.
- D) It promotes sustainable development.

Analysis: The correct one is C. It mentions globalization has generated significant inequalities, while the other options do not reflect negative consequences according to the text.

#7: Technology

Artificial intelligence (AI) is revolutionizing numerous fields, from medicine to engineering. Advanced algorithms analyze large volumes of content to capture patterns and make accurate predictions. However, the rapid adoption of AI raises ethical concerns, such as privacy and potential bias in algorithms. It is crucial to develop regulatory frameworks that ensure the ethical and equitable use of AI.

#7: What is one of the ethical concerns associated with artificial intelligence according to the passage?

- A) The ability to make accurate predictions
- B) The revolution in the field of medicine
- C) Privacy
- D) The identification of patterns in large volumes of content

Analysis: The correct one is C. It highlights privacy as an ethical concern associated with artificial intelligence. The other options are not mentioned as ethical concerns.

#8: Education

Online education has gained popularity, especially during the COVID-19 pandemic. This format offers flexibility and accessibility, allowing students to learn at their own pace and from anywhere, it presents challenges, such as a lack of face-to-face interaction and difficulty maintaining motivation. To maximize the benefits of online education, it is important to integrate interactive methods and ongoing support.

#8: According to the passage, what is one of the challenges of online education?

- A) Flexibility in learning
- B) Accessibility for all students
- C) Lack of face-to-face interaction
- D) Possibility of learning from anywhere

Analysis: The correct one is C. It mentions the lack of face-to-face interaction as one of the challenges of online education, while the other options mention benefits.

#9: Health

Regular exercise is essential to maintain good physical and mental health. Studies have shown that physical activity strengthens the cardiovascular and musculoskeletal system, reduces stress, and improves mood. At least 150 minutes of moderate exercise per week is recommended to obtain these benefits. Incorporating exercise into your daily routine is challenging, but the long-term benefits make it a worthwhile investment.

#9: What is one of the benefits of regular exercise according to the passage?

- A) It strengthens the cardiovascular system.

- B) It increases stress.

- C) It decreases muscle mass.

- D) It requires less than 100 minutes per week.

Analysis: The correct one is A. It mentions that regular exercise strengthens the cardiovascular system, while the other options do not mention benefits.

#10: Culture

Contemporary art challenges traditional notions of aesthetics and artistic value. Artists like Banksy and Yayoi Kusama use unconventional and innovative mediums to express social and political messages. This approach has sparked a debate about what constitutes art and who decides its value. Accessibility and interaction with the public are key aspects that distinguish contemporary art from traditional art.

 # 10: According to the passage, what aspect distinguishes contemporary art from traditional art?

- A) Use of conventional means

- B) Focus on social and political messages

- C) Adoption of traditional techniques

- D) Lack of interaction with the public

Analysis: The correct one is B. It mentions that contemporary art is distinguished by its focus on social and political messages, while the other options do not reflect this distinction.

Compendium 2

#11: History

The Renaissance, which began in Italy in the 14th century and spread across Europe in the 15th and 16th centuries, marked an era of great advances in the arts, science, and human thought. Artists like Leonardo da Vinci and Michelangelo revolutionized painting and sculpture, while scientists like Galileo and Copernicus challenged established beliefs about the universe. This period saw the rise of humanism, a philosophy that emphasized the value and capacity of the human being.

#11: According to the passage, what aspect of the Renaissance challenged established beliefs about the universe?

- A) The rise of humanism

- B) The works of Leonardo da Vinci

- C) The scientific discoveries of Galileo and Copernicus

- D) Michelangelo's sculpture

Analysis: The correct one is C. It indicates that scientists Galileo and Copernicus challenged established beliefs about the universe during the Renaissance.

#12: Science

DNA, or deoxyribonucleic acid, is the molecule that contains genetic information in living beings. Its double helix structure, discovered by James Watson and Francis Crick in 1953, allows precise replication of genetic material during cell division. Mutations in DNA lead to genetic diseases, but are a source of genetic variability that drives evolution. Advances in sequencing technology have made it possible to map entire genomes, opening new frontiers in personalized medicine.

#12: What allowed the double helix structure of DNA according to the passage?

- A) Genetic variability

- B) The appearance of genetic diseases

- C) The precise replication of genetic material

- D) The mapping of complete genomes

Analysis: The correct one is C. It explains that the double helix structure of DNA allows precise replication of genetic material during cell division. The other options do not relate to this function of the double helix structure.

#13: Literature

Emily Dickinson's poetry, often characterized by her innovative use of language and punctuation, offers a profound exploration of themes such as death, nature, and immortality. His poems, many of which were published after his death, challenge the poetic conventions of his time with their freestyle and intense introspection. Dickinson's work has been the subject of extensive critical analysis, revealing layers of meaning and emotion in her brief but powerful compositions.

#13: What characterizes Emily Dickinson's poetry according to the passage?

- A) Its narrative style is extensive.

- B) She uses intense introspection and innovative language.

- C) It lacks critical analysis.

- D) It focuses on everyday life.

Analysis: The correct one is B. It mentions that Emily Dickinson's poetry is characterized by her intense introspection and her innovative use of language and punctuation. The other options do not describe his poetry.

#14: Environment

Coral reefs, often called the "jungles of the sea," are diverse marine ecosystems that are home to thousands of species. These ecosystems are essential to the health of the oceans, providing habitats, protecting coastlines from erosion, and supporting fisheries. However, coral reefs are threatened by climate change, pollution, and overfishing. Conservation of these ecosystems requires global efforts, including reducing greenhouse gas emissions and creating marine protected areas.

#14: According to the passage, what role do coral reefs play?

- A) They increase coastal erosion.
- B) They house a few marine species.
- C) They protect the coasts from erosion.
- D) They reduce greenhouse gas emissions.

Analysis: The correct one is C. It indicates that coral reefs protect coasts from erosion, among other essential functions.

#15: Psychology

The phenomenon of impostor syndrome refers to the persistent feeling of not deserving the achievements achieved, despite evidence of success. People who experience this syndrome often attribute their success to luck or external factors, and fear being exposed as "frauds." This phenomenon is common among successful professionals and high-achieving students and leads to high levels of stress and anxiety. Cognitive behavioral therapy helps people challenge these negative thoughts.

#15: What does imposter syndrome refer to according to the passage?

- A) The inability to achieve success
- B) The attribution of success to luck or external factors
- C) Public recognition of achievements
- D) The lack of stress and anxiety

Analysis: The correct one is B. It describes imposter syndrome as the attribution of success to luck or external factors and the fear of being exposed as fraud.

#16: Economy

The concept of the circular economy seeks to redefine growth, focusing on positive benefits for all of society. Unlike the traditional linear model of "take, make, waste," the circular economy is based on three principles: eliminating waste and pollution, keeping products and materials in use, and regenerating natural systems. This reduces pressure on the environment and offers new opportunities for economic growth and employment.

#16: What is one of the principles of the circular economy according to the passage?

- A) It increases waste production.
- B) It maintains products and materials in use.
- C) It reduces economic growth.
- D) It promotes the traditional linear model.

Analysis: The correct one is B. It mentions that one of the principles of the circular economy is to keep products and materials in use.

#17: Technology

The development of blockchain technology has revolutionized the way digital transactions are managed and recorded. By providing a decentralized and secure structure, blockchain enables the creation of immutable records that are transparent and accessible to all participants. This technology has applications beyond cryptocurrencies, including supply chain management, identity verification, and protection. Blockchain adoption faces challenges, such as scalability and energy consumption.

#17: According to the passage, what is one of the applications of blockchain technology?

- A) The production of cryptocurrencies
- B) Supply chain management
- C) The increase in energy consumption
- D) Centralization

Analysis: The correct one is B. Mention that one of the applications of blockchain technology is supply chain management. The other options do not reflect the applications mentioned.

#18: Education

Inclusive education is based on the principle that all students, regardless of their abilities or disabilities, should have access to quality education in common environments. This involves adapting teaching methods, educational materials, and the physical environment to meet diverse needs. Inclusive education promotes equal opportunities and prepares all students to participate in society. However, its effective implementation requires commitment and continuous training on the part of educators.

#18: According to the passage, what does inclusive education entail?

- A) It separates students with disabilities.
- B) It adapts teaching methods and educational materials.
- C) It reduces equality of opportunity.
- D) It limits participation in the company.

Analysis: The correct one is B. It mentions that inclusive education involves adapting teaching methods and educational materials to meet the diverse needs of students.

#19: Health

Nutrition plays a crucial role in maintaining health and preventing disease. A balanced diet that includes a variety of essential nutrients strengthens the immune system, improves cognitive function, and reduces the risk of chronic diseases such as diabetes and heart disease. In addition, healthy eating habits contribute to mental well-being, reducing stress and improving mood. Encouraging proper nutrition from an early age is essential to developing healthy habits.

#19: What is one of the benefits of a balanced diet according to the passage?

- A) It increases the risk of chronic diseases.
- B) It improves cognitive function.
- C) It weakens the immune system.
- D) It increases stress and reduces mood.

Analysis: The correct one is B. It mentions that a balanced diet improves cognitive function, among other benefits.

#20: Sociology

Social mobility refers to the ability of an individual or group to move up or down the socioeconomic structure of a society. Education, employment and government policies are key factors influencing social mobility. In societies with high social mobility, individuals have greater opportunities to improve their economic and social situation through merit and effort. However, structural barriers, such as unequal access to education and employment, limit social mobility and perpetuate inequality.

#20: What influences social mobility depending on the passage?

- A) Permanence in the same social class
- B) Inequality of access to education and employment
- C) Lack of merit and effort
- D) The immutable socioeconomic structure

Analysis: The correct one is B. It mentions that inequality in access to education and employment limits social mobility.

#21: Art

Abstract art, which developed in the early 20th century, seeks to represent concepts and emotions rather than imitate reality. Artists such as Wassily Kandinsky and Piet Mondrian explored shapes, colors, and lines to express feelings and ideas in a non-representational way. Abstract art allows for a personal and subjective interpretation, inviting the viewer to find their meaning in the work. This art form has influenced numerous subsequent art movements and remains an integral part of the contemporary art scene.

#21: What does abstract art seek to represent according to the passage?

- A) Objective reality
- B) Concepts and emotions
- C) Scenes from everyday life
- D) Detailed human figures

Analysis: The correct one is B. It mentions that abstract art seeks to represent concepts and emotions rather than imitate reality.

#22: Technology

Artificial intelligence (AI) is transforming various sectors, from health to transportation. In medicine, AI records patterns and diagnoses diseases with astonishing accuracy. In transportation, autonomous vehicles, controlled by AI systems, promise to reduce traffic accidents and improve travel efficiency, the implementation of AI poses ethical and privacy challenges, as adequate regulation is required to protect the rights of individuals.

#22: What is one of the challenges posed by artificial intelligence according to the passage?

- A) Improving travel efficiency
- B) The reduction of traffic accidents
- C) Ethical and privacy challenges
- D) Accuracy in the diagnosis of diseases

Analysis: The correct one is C. It mentions that artificial intelligence poses ethical and privacy challenges, among other benefits and applications.

#23: Philosophy

Existentialism is a philosophical movement that emphasizes freedom and individual responsibility, affirming that human beings create the meaning of their lives through their actions and decisions. Philosophers such as Jean-Paul Sartre and Simone de Beauvoir argued that, in the absence of a predefined purpose, individuals must take responsibility for giving meaning to their existence. This philosophy addresses the anguish and alienation that arise from the awareness of absolute freedom and lack of certainties.

#23: According to the passage, what does existentialism emphasize?

- A) The lack of individual responsibility
- B) The existence of a predefined purpose
- C) Freedom and individual responsibility
- D) The elimination of anxiety and alienation

Analysis: The correct one is C. It says that existentialism emphasizes freedom and individual responsibility.

#24: Science

The theory of evolution by natural selection, proposed by Charles Darwin, revolutionized our understanding of biodiversity. According to this theory, organisms with characteristics that give them an advantage in their environment are more likely to survive and reproduce; these favorable characteristics become more common in the population. Evolution is not a linear or directed process, it is a series of gradual changes driven by genetic variability and adaptation to the environment.

#24: What does the theory of evolution by natural selection suggest according to the passage?

- A) The elimination of genetic variability

- B) The random reproduction of organisms

- C) The survival and reproduction of organisms with advantageous characteristics

- D) Lack of adaptation to the environment

Analysis: The correct one is C. It explains that the theory of evolution by natural selection suggests that organisms with advantageous characteristics are more likely to survive and reproduce.

#25: Literature

George Orwell's novel "1984" presents a dystopian vision of a totalitarian future where the government, known as Big Brother, controls every aspect of citizens' lives. The manipulation of the truth, constant surveillance, and the suppression of individuality are central themes in the work. Orwell wrote "1984" as a warning about the dangers of authoritarianism and the loss of personal freedoms, using his narrative to explore the extreme consequences of a totalitarian state.

#25: What central theme is presented in George Orwell's novel "1984" according to the passage?

- A) The liberation of citizens

- B) Constant surveillance and manipulation of the truth

- C) Economic prosperity

- D) Freedom of expression

Analysis: The correct one is B. Explain that the novel "1984" presents themes such as constant surveillance and manipulation of the truth. The other options do not reflect the central themes of the work.

#26: History

The Industrial Revolution, which began in Great Britain in the 18th century, transformed the economy and society profoundly. The introduction of mass-production machinery increased efficiency and productivity, leading to the growth of cities and the expansion of trade, this period brought with it challenges such as labor exploitation, unsanitary conditions in factories, and growing social inequality. Labor movements and legislative reforms emerged as responses to these problems.

#26: What effect did the Industrial Revolution have according to the passage?

- A) The decrease in productivity
- B) The reduction of trade
- C) The growth of cities and the expansion of commerce
- D) The elimination of social inequality

Analysis: The correct one is C. It mentions that the Industrial Revolution led to the growth of cities and the expansion of commerce.

#27: Environment

Deforestation, driven by agricultural expansion, logging, and urban development, is one of the main threats to global biodiversity. Forests are home to a wide variety of animal and plant species, and their destruction leads to the loss of habitats, the extinction of species, and the imbalance of ecosystems. Forest conservation is essential to protect biodiversity, mitigate climate change, and maintain ecosystem services that benefit humanity.

#27: What effect does deforestation have according to the passage?

- A) The creation of new habitats
- B) The increase in biodiversity
- C) The loss of habitats and the extinction of species
- D) The stabilization of ecosystems

Analysis: The correct one is C. It mentions that deforestation leads to the loss of habitats and the extinction of species.

#28: Sociology

The concept of social capital refers to the resources and benefits that individuals obtain through their social networks and relationships. These connections provide emotional support, valuable information, and economic opportunities. Social capital strengthens communities by fostering trust and cooperation among its members.

The lack of social capital limits access to these advantages and perpetuates social and economic inequality.

#28: What does social capital provide according to the passage?

- A) Economic disadvantages
- B) Valuable information and emotional support
- C) Distrust among community members
- D) Social isolation

Analysis: The correct one is B. It explains that social capital provides valuable information, emotional support, and economic opportunities.

29: Health

Mental health is a fundamental aspect of overall well-being and affects how we think, feel, and act. Factors such as stress, trauma, and genetics influence mental health. Mental illnesses, such as depression and anxiety, are common and treatable, but they are often surrounded by stigmas that prevent people from seeking help. Access to mental health services and social support are crucial to recovery and maintenance of mental well-being.

#29: What is mentioned in the passage as a factor influencing mental health?

- A) Economic stability
- B) Genetics and stress
- C) Social popularity
- D) Academic education

Analysis: The correct one is B. It explains that factors such as genetics and stress influence mental health.

#30: Technology

Robotics has advanced in recent decades, with applications ranging from manufacturing to medicine. Robots perform repetitive and dangerous tasks with precision and efficiency, freeing humans for more creative and strategic work. In medicine, surgical robots allow complex operations to be performed with high precision, reducing the risk of complications. However, the integration of robots into the workforce raises questions about job displacement and the need for new skills.

#30: What is the application of robotics in medicine according to the passage?

- A) It performs repetitive tasks in manufacturing.
- B) It allows complex surgical operations with high precision.
- C) It displaces human jobs in the workforce.
- D) It increases creativity at work.

Analysis: The correct one is B. It mentions that surgical robots allow complex operations to be performed with high precision in medicine. The other options do not reflect the applications mentioned.

Chapter 6: Mathematics Mastery

Now it is time to master the Mathematics section. To make your task easier, you will find three main divisions in this chapter, each containing the concepts you need to review. At the end of each division, there are exercises and mini-tests to do:

Pre-Algebra and Elementary Algebra

These topics form the foundation upon which more advanced mathematical concepts are built. Without a solid understanding of operations with whole numbers, fractions, and decimals, it is easy to make basic mistakes.

I encourage you to engage with these concepts to develop critical problem-solving skills:

Operations With Whole Numbers

When adding integers with the same sign, add their absolute values and keep the sign. For example, -5 + (-3), add the values (5+3), obtaining 8, and since both numbers are negative, the result is -8.

When subtracting, add the opposite of the number you are subtracting, as in 7 - (-2) becomes 7 + 2, which gives 9.

Multiplication and division follow specific rules: same signs result in a positive answer (e.g., -4 * -3 = 12, 20 / 5 = 4); different signs result in a negative answer (e.g., -6 * 2 = -12, -15 / 3 = -5).

Follow the order of operations: parentheses first, then exponents, multiplication and division from left to right, and addition and subtraction from left to right. This sequence ensures accurate calculations.

Operations With Fractions and Decimals

To add or subtract fractions, find a common denominator. For example, to add 1/4 and 1/6, the common denominator is 12. Convert both: 1/4 becomes 3/12 and 1/6 becomes 2/12. Then add the numerators, obtaining 5/12.

Multiplication of fractions involves multiplying numerators and denominators (e.g., 2/3 * 3/4 = 6/12, simplified to 1/2). To divide fractions, invert the divisor and multiply (e.g., 2/3 ÷ 3/4 becomes 2/3 * 4/3 = 8/9).

For decimals, align them by the decimal point before adding or subtracting (e.g., 2.35 + 1.6 = 3.95). When multiplying, ignore decimals and then place the dot in the correct place in the final result (e.g., 2.5 * 3.2 = 8.00). For division, move the decimal of the divisor to the right until it is a whole number and move the decimal of the dividend to the same number of places.

Simplify whenever possible and double-check calculations for accuracy.

Ratios, Proportions, and Percentages

Ratios compare two quantities. if you have 3 apples and 2 oranges, the ratio is 3:2. To solve problems with proportions, such as finding the number of oranges if you have 6 apples, use an equivalent proportion. State the proportion 3/2 = 6/x, then solve by crossing the products: 3x = 12. Divide 12 by 3, obtaining x = 4.

Percentages represent a part of 100. To find 20% of 50, convert the percentage to a decimal: (20% is 0.20) and multiply (50 * 0.20 = 10). To find what percentage 25 is of 50, divide 25 by 50 and multiply by 100, getting 50%.

Powers and Square Roots

Powers involve raising one number to another. For example, 2^3 means 2 multiplied by itself 3 times, resulting in 8. Find out the base and exponent correctly. If the exponent is negative, as in 2^{-3}, convert the power to a fraction: 1/ (2^3), resulting in 1/8.

Square roots are the inverse of squaring. The square root of 9 is 3 because 3^2 is 9. To solve for $\sqrt{25}$, think about what number multiplied by itself is 25, which is 5. Don't forget there could be a negative root, like -5 because $(-5)^2$ is also 25.

In combination problems, such as solving $4^2 - \sqrt{16}$, you solve for the power, getting 16, and then the square root, which is 4. The result is 16 - 4, equal to 12.

Least Common Multiple and Greatest Common Divisor

The least common multiple (LCM) of two numbers is the smallest number divisible by both.

To find the LCM of 12 and 15, decompose the numbers into prime factors: 12 should be $2^2 * 3$, and 15 is $3 * 5$. Take the largest exponent of each prime factor: 2^2, 3, and 5; multiply these factors: $2^2 * 3 * 5 = 60$. The LCM of 12 and 15 is 60.

The greatest common factor (GCD) is the greatest number that divides both numbers without leaving a remainder. To find the GCF of 12 and 15, decompose the numbers into prime factors: 12 is $2^2 * 3$, and 15 is $3 * 5$. Take the common factors with the lowest exponent: just 3. The GCF of 12 and 15 is 3.

Always verify each step. If you work with large numbers, use Euclid's algorithm for the GCF: divide the larger number by the smaller one and continue until the remainder is 0, with the last divisor being the GCD.

Algebraic Expressions

They combine numbers, variables, and operations. $3x + 2$ is an expression where x is the variable. Simplify expressions by combining like terms: in $2x + 3x - 4$, combine $2x$ and $3x$ to get $5x - 4$.

When expanding, use the distributive property. To expand $2(x + 3)$, multiply 2 by each term inside the parentheses: $2x + 6$. In factoring, take the common factor: In $3x + 6$, the common factor is 3, resulting in $3(x + 2)$.

Practice combining like terms and use the distributive property and factoring to simplify and solve expressions.

Linear Equations of One Variable

For this, you must find the value of the variable that makes the equation true. In the case of $2x + 5 = 17$, subtract 5 from both sides to get $2x = 12$. Then, divide both sides by 2 to find $x = 6$. This process is simple but requires precision at each step.

To make it practical, when solving $3x - 7 = 8$, add 7 to both sides to get $3x = 15$, then divide by 3 to find $x = 5$.

Perform the same operation on both sides. When facing equations with fractions, such as $(1/2) x + 4 = 7$, subtract 4 from both sides to get $(1/2) x = 3$. Then, multiply both sides by 2 to find $x = 6$.

In one like $5x + 3 = 2x + 9$, subtract $2x$ from both sides to get $3x + 3 = 9$. Then, subtract 3 from both sides to get $3x = 6$. Divide both sides by 3 to find $x = 2$.

Linear Inequalities of One Variable

These use inequality signs ($>$, $<$, $\geq$, $\leq$) instead of an equality sign. When solving $3x - 4 > 5$, add 4 to both sides to get $3x > 9$. Then, divide both sides by 3 to find $x > 3$. Remember that when multiplying or dividing both sides by a negative number, the inequality sign is reversed. For $-2x < 8$, dividing by -2 gives $x > -4$.

In this case: $2x + 3 \leq 7$, subtract 3 from both sides to get $2x \leq 4$. Then, divide by 2 to find $x \leq 2$. Practicing helps you understand how operations affect the direction of inequality and develop a strategy for solving these problems efficiently.

Another might be to solve $4x - 5 \geq 3x + 2$. Subtract $3x$ from both sides to get $x - 5 \geq 2$. Then, add 5 to both sides to find $x \geq 7$. Check each step and see how the basic operations affect the inequality.

Systems of Linear Equations

It consists of finding the values of the variables that satisfy all equations simultaneously, as in the system: $2x + y = 5 \quad x - y = 1$

To resolve it, use the substitution or elimination method.

With the replacement, clear one and substitute it in the other. For example, from the second equation, $x = y + 1$. Substituting into the first, $2(y + 1) + y = 5$, results in $2y + 2 + y = 5$. Simplify to $3y + 2 = 5$ and subtract 2 on both sides, getting $3y = 3$, then divide by 3 to get $y = 1$. Substituting $y = 1$ into $x = y + 1$, you get $x = 2$.

Elimination consists of adding or subtracting to eliminate a variable. Adding the two original equations gives $3x = 6$, and dividing by 3 gives $x = 2$. Substituting $x = 2$ into $x - y = 1$ gives $2 - y = 1$, and solving for y gives $y = 1$.

Properties of Numbers (Associative, Commutative, Distributive)

The associative property groups numbers without changing the result, as in $(a + b) + c = a + (b + c)$. If you have $2 + (3 + 4)$, calculate $2 + 7$ or $5 + 4$, both equal 9.

The commutative indicates changes in the order without changing the result, as in $a + b = b + a$. For example, $3 + 5$ is the same as $5 + 3$, both equal 8.

The distributive combines addition and multiplication: $a(b + c) = ab + ac$. If you calculate $3(2 + 4)$, you could first add (6) and then multiply by 3, getting 18. Alternatively, by multiplying: $3 * 2 + 3 * 4$, you get $6 + 12$, which is also 18.

These properties are important when simplifying and solving equations, when simplifying $2(x + 3) - x$, use the distributive to get $2x + 6 - x$, then combine like terms to get $x + 6$.

Intermediate Algebra and Coordinate Geometry

These topics prepare you to handle quadratic equations, and systems of nonlinear equations, among other aspects, which are more advanced concepts for the exam. Reviewing the topics allows you to apply algebraic and geometric concepts effectively:

Quadratic Equations

They are equations of the form $ax^2 + bx + c = 0$, where a, b, and c are constants and x is the variable. A common method to solve them is using the quadratic formula: $x = (-b \pm \sqrt{b^2 - 4ac}) / 2a$.

For example, to solve $2x^2 - 4x - 6 = 0$, identify a = 2, b = -4, and c = -6. Substitute these values into the formula: $x = (4 \pm \sqrt{(-4)^2 - 4 * 2 * (-6)}) / (2 * 2)$. Simplify within the root: $x = (4 \pm \sqrt{16 + 48}) / 4$. Then, $x = (4 \pm \sqrt{64}) / 4$.

This results in $x = (4 \pm 8) / 4$, get two solutions: x = 3 and x = -1/2.

In these cases, avoid errors such as forgetting the $\pm$ sign and ensure not to simplify prematurely.

Functions and Their Graphics

Functions represent relationships between inputs and outputs, graphically represented. For example, the function $f(x) = 2x + 3$ is a straight line. To graph it, find two points: if x = 0, then f (0) = 3; if x = 1, then f (1) = 5. Draw the line through these points.

Another example is the quadratic function $f(x) = x^2 - 4$. Find the vertex (0, -4) and additional points such as (1, -3) and (-1, -3).

Quadratic Inequalities

Quadratic inequalities are of the form $ax^2 + bx + c > 0$ (o < 0, $\geq$ 0, $\leq$ 0). Solving them consists of finding the intervals where the inequality is true.

For $2x^2 - 3x - 2 > 0$, solve the equation $2x^2 - 3x - 2 = 0$. Using the quadratic formula, find the roots: $x = (3 \pm \sqrt{9 + 16}) / 4$. This gives $x = (3 \pm 5) / 4$, resulting in x = 2 and x = -1/2. These roots divide the number line into intervals.

Test a value in each interval to determine where the inequality is true. If x = 0 on (-∞, -1/2), $2(0)^2 - 3(0) - 2 = -2 < 0$. Continue testing values on other intervals to find the solution.

Polynomials and Factoring

Polynomials are algebraic expressions consisting of terms of the form ax^n, where a is a coefficient, x is a variable, and n is an exponent. To factor them you have to decompose them into products of simpler factors.

In this case, to factor $x^2 + 5x + 6$, find two numbers that multiply to 6 and add to 5. These are 2 and 3, thus, $x^2 + 5x + 6$ factors as (x + 2) (x + 3).

An example of this is factoring $3x^2 - 12x$. Here, the common factor $3x$ could be taken out, resulting in $3x(x - 4)$. Check the factors by re-multiplying them to verify that the original polynomial is obtained.

Rational Expressions

They are fractions where the numerator and/or denominator are polynomials. Simplifying them is finding common factors and canceling them.

For instance, to simplify $(x^2 - 4)/(x^2 - x - 6)$, factor both the numerator and the denominator: $(x + 2)(x - 2) / (x - 3)(x + 2)$. Then, cancel the common factor $(x + 2)$, resulting in $(x - 2)/(x - 3)$.

The solution might involve finding a common denominator, to solve $1/(x + 2) + 1/(x - 2) = 1/2$, multiply both sides by the common denominator $(x + 2)(x - 2)$ and simplify, check the solutions in the original equation to avoid values that make the denominator zero.

Exponential and Logarithmic Equations

Exponential equations have the variable in the exponent, while logarithmic equations have it inside a logarithm. To solve an exponential equation like $2^x = 8$, rewrite 8 as a power of 2, that is, $2^x = 2^3$, which implies $x = 3$. For a logarithmic one like $\log(x) = 3$, rewrite in exponential form: $x = 10^3$, so $x = 1000$.

Combining properties of exponents and logarithms simplifies equations. For example, solving $3^x = 27$ leads you to rewrite 27 as 3^3, resulting in $x = 3$.

Systems of Nonlinear Equations

This includes at least one equation that is not a straight line. You should find the values of the variables that satisfy all the equations simultaneously. Substitution or equalization is common for this purpose.

For example, consider the system:

$y = x^2 + 2x + 1$

$y = 3x + 2$

To find the solutions, equate the equations:

$x^2 + 2x + 1 = 3x + 2$

Simplify:

$x^2 + 2x + 1 - 3x - 2 = 0$

$x^2 - x - 1 = 0$

To solve the quadratic equation, use the general formula:

$$x = \frac{-b \pm \sqrt{b^2 - 4ac}}{2a}$$

Here, a = 1, b = -1, and c = -1:

$$x = \frac{1 \pm \sqrt{5}}{2}$$

Then, substitute the values of x into the original equations to find y.

Properties and Operations With Matrices

A matrix is an arrangement of numbers organized in rows and columns. Basic operations include addition, subtraction, and matrix multiplication. Consider matrices A and B:

A = [1 2]

[3. 4]

B = [5 6]

[7 8]

The sum A + B is made by adding the corresponding elements:

A + B = [6 8]

[10 12]

Matrix multiplication involves multiplying rows by columns and summing the products. If A is mxn and B is nxp, the product AB results in mxp.

Distance Between Two Points on the Plane

The distance between two points (x1, y1) and (x2, y2) on a plane is calculated using the distance formula:

$$d = \sqrt{(x_2 - x_1)^2 + (y_2 - y_1)^2}$$

To find the distance between (3, 4) and (7, 1):

$$d = \sqrt{(7 - 3)^2 + (1 - 4)^2}$$

$$d = \sqrt{16 + 9}$$

$$d = \sqrt{25}$$

$$d = 5$$

Apply it to calculate the distance between points on the plane.

Slope of a Straight Line

The slope of a line measures its inclination. It is calculated using two points on the line, applying the formula:

$m = (y2 - y1) / (x2 - x1)$

Here, m represents the slope, (x1, y1) and (x2, y2) are the points on the line. If (2, 3) and (4, 7) are used, the slope is calculated as:

$m = (7 - 3) / (4 - 2) = 4 / 2 = 2$

This indicates that for every unit that the line advances horizontally, it goes up two units vertically. A positive slope means the line goes up to the right, while a negative slope means the line goes down to the right.

Equation of the Line

The equation of a line is expressed in several forms, the most common being the point-slope form and the slope-intercept form. The point-slope form is used when a point on the line and its slope are known:

$y - y1 = m (x - x1)$

If the slope m is 2 and the known is (3, 5), the equation becomes:

$y - 5 = 2(x - 3)$

Simplifying, we obtain:

$y - 5 = 2x - 6$

$y = 2x - 1$

This is equivalent to slope-intercept form, where the equation of the line is expressed as:

$y = mx + b$

In the example above, the slope m is 2 and the y-intercept b is -1.

Geometric Transformations (Translation, Reflection, Rotation, Dilation)

Geometric transformations alter the position or size of a figure in the plane. There are several types:

- **Translation:** Move each point in the figure the same distance in a specific direction. For example, translating (2, 3) 5 units to the right and 2 up results in (7, 5).
- **Reflection:** Reflect a figure about an axis, creating a mirror image. Reflecting the point (4, 2) on the y-axis gives the (-4, 2).

- **Rotation:** Rotate a figure around a fixed point, usually the origin. Rotating the point (1, 2) 90 degrees counterclockwise around the origin gives the (-2, 1).
- **Dilation:** Changes the size of the figure, increasing or decreasing its scale. Dilating (3, 4) by a scale factor of 2 results in (6, 8).

Be careful to apply the formulas and procedures correctly to avoid errors and do not make mistakes such as applying the scale factor in dilation or not following the correct direction in a translation.

Plane Geometry and Trigonometry

Knowledge in this segment is essential for the mathematics section of the ACT. It includes the study of angles, triangles, circles, and solids, as well as trigonometric functions and their applications.

Angles and Their Measurements

They are a fundamental part of geometry and are measured in degrees. A straight one measures 90 degrees, an acute angle measures less than 90 degrees, and an obtuse one measures more than 90 degrees but less than 180 degrees. The measurement is calculated using various tools, such as a protractor, or mathematical formulas.

To calculate the value of an angle inside a triangle, use the rule that the sum of the interior angles is always 180 degrees. For example, if two angles of a triangle are 45 degrees and 55 degrees, the third is calculated like this:

45 + 55 + x = 180

100 + x = 180

x = 80 degrees

Supplementary angles are those that add up to 180 degrees. If one angle measures 120 degrees, its supplementary is:

180 - 120 = 60 degrees.

Properties of Triangles (Isosceles, Equilateral, Right Angles)

An equilateral angle has three sides and three equal angles of 60 degrees each. In an isosceles, at least two sides are equal and the opposites of these sides are equal.

To calculate their properties, various formulas are used. In a right triangle, the Pythagorean theorem is fundamental: $a^2 + b^2 = c^2$, where c is the hypotenuse, and a and b are the other two sides. If the sides a and b are 3 and 4 units respectively, the hypotenuse c is calculated as follows:

$3^2 + 4^2 = c^2$

$9 + 16 = c^2$

$25 = c^2$

$c = 5$

In an isosceles, if the equal sides measure 5 units and the angle between them is 40 degrees, trigonometry is used to find the base and other angles.

Properties of Circles

The radius is the distance from the center of the circle to any point on its edge. The diameter is twice the radius and passes through the center of the circle. The circumference is the distance around the circle and is calculated as $C = 2\pi r$, where r is the radius. The area of the circle is calculated as $A = \pi r^2$.

If the radius of a circle is 3, the diameter will be twice this:

Diameter = 2 * 3 = 6

The circumference is calculated as:

$C = 2\pi * 3 \approx 18.85$

The area is calculated as:

$A = \pi * 3^2 \approx 28.27$

Remember that π (pi) is approximately 3.14159. Avoid confusing radius with diameter, resulting in incorrect calculations.

Relationships Between Angles and Arcs of a Circle

In a circle, angles and arcs have specific relationships. A central angle is one whose vertex is at the center of the circle and its sides are radii of the circle. The measurement of a central one is equal to the measurement of the arc that it intercepts.

Another concept is the inscribed angle, which is one whose vertex is on the edge of the circle and whose sides are chords of the circle. The measure of one inscribed is half the measure of the arc that it intercepts. If it intercepts an arc of 80 degrees, the inscribed measures 40 degrees.

Areas and Perimeters of Polygons

They are closed plane figures with several straight sides. Common polygons include triangles, squares, rectangles, pentagons, and hexagons.

The perimeter of a polygon is the sum of the lengths of all its sides, so for a square with sides of length 4, the perimeter is calculated by adding the four sides:

Perimeter = 4 + 4 + 4 + 4 = 16

The area of a polygon is determined in different ways depending on the shape. For a rectangle, multiply the length by the width. For a triangle, the formula A = 1/2 * base * height is used. If the base is 5 and its height is 6:

Area = 1/2 * 5 * 6 = 15

In the case of regular polygons, where all sides and angles are equal, specific formulas are used. The area of a regular hexagon is found by dividing it into six equilateral triangles and adding their areas.

Always check that the dimensions are in the same units before calculating.

Volumes and Surface Areas of Solids

This includes three-dimensional figures such as cubes, prisms, cylinders, cones, spheres, and pyramids. Volume measures the space within a solid, while surface area measures the sum of the areas of all the faces of the solid.

To calculate the volume of a cube, raise the length of one of its sides to the cube. If a cube has sides of length 3:

Volume = 3^3 = 27

The surface area is found by adding the area of all the faces. In the case of the cube, it has six equal faces:

Surface area = 6 * (side²) = 6 * (3^2) = 54

For a cylinder, the volume is calculated by multiplying the area of the base by the height ($V = \pi r^2 h$). If the radius of the base is 2 and the height is 5:

Volume = π * 2^2 * 5 = $20\pi \approx$ 62.83

The surface area of a cylinder includes the areas of the two circular bases and the lateral surface:

Surface area = $2\pi r^2 + 2\pi rh$

Practice with a variety of solids and review the steps for each calculation.

Fundamental Trigonometric Identities

They are relationships existing between trigonometric functions and are essential to simplify expressions and solve trigonometric equations.

Basic identities include the Pythagorean identity: $\sin^2(\theta) + \cos^2(\theta) = 1$. This identity, derived from the Pythagorean theorem, is useful for finding a trigonometric value when another is known.

If sin(θ) = 3/5, we find cos(θ) using the Pythagorean identity:

$\cos^2(\theta) = 1 - \sin^2(\theta)$

$\cos^2(\theta) = 1 - (3/5)^2$

$\cos^2(\theta) = 1 - 9/25$

$\cos^2(\theta) = 16/25$

$\cos(\theta) = \pm\sqrt{(16/25)}$

$\cos(\theta) = \pm 4/5$

Another example is the tangent identity: tan(θ) = sin(θ)/cos(θ). This relationship is useful for converting between trigonometric functions and simplifying calculations. Confusion about identities, such as sin (90° - θ) = cos(θ) and cos (90° - θ) = sin(θ), is necessary to solve problems involving complementary angles.

Trigonometric Functions and Their Graphs

Trigonometric functions, such as sine, cosine, and tangent, describe relationships between angles and sides of a right triangle, fundamental in trigonometry. These functions are represented graphically, showing how they vary with angles.

The sine function (sin(θ)) represents the relationship between the length of the leg opposite the angle θ and the hypotenuse in a right triangle. Its graph is a sine wave oscillating between -1 and 1.

The cosine function (cos(θ)) has a similar graph but shifted 90 degrees, starting at 1 when θ is 0.

The tangent function (tan(θ)) is defined as the quotient between the sine and the cosine and has vertical asymptotes at the points where the cosine is zero. To graph them, knowing their periods and amplitudes is useful.

Law of Sines and Cosines

They are powerful tools in trigonometry, especially useful for solving oblique triangles, that is, those that do not have a right angle.

The law of sines establishes a relationship between the sides of a triangle and their opposite angles: a/sin(A) = b/sin(B) = c/sin(C). This formula allows finding an unknown side or angle when the other values are known.

Imagine a triangle with sides a, b, and c, and angles A, B, and C opposite these sides respectively. If two angles and one side are known (e.g., A, B, and C), use the law of sines to find the other sides:

b/sin(B) = a/sin(A)

b = a * sin(B) / sin(A)

On the other hand, the law of cosines is useful when knowing two sides and the included angle, or all three sides of the triangle. The formula is: $c^2 = a^2 + b^2 - 2ab * \cos(C)$.

Now, for a triangle with sides a, b, and c, and angle C between a, and b. If you know a, b, and C, find c:

$c^2 = a^2 + b^2 - 2ab * \cos(C)$

$c = \sqrt{(a^2 + b^2 - 2ab * \cos(C))}$

Applications of Trigonometry to Real Life Problems

Trigonometry has practical applications in various fields such as physics, engineering, and architecture. It is used to determine the heights of inaccessible objects, such as buildings or mountains.

For example, to find the height of a building, if you are a distance away and measure an elevation angle θ from the ground to the top of the building, use the tangent to find the height h: $\tan(\theta) = h/d$, so $h = d * \tan(\theta)$.

Another common use is in navigation and astronomy to calculate distances and positions of stars and planets Navigators use it to determine exact positions at sea using longitude, latitude, and the elevation angle of stars. In construction, it helps calculate ramp and roof inclinations for stability and safety.

Practice Questions and Mini Tests

Practice Questions: Pre-Algebra and Elementary Algebra

Operations with whole numbers

1. Simplify: 15 - 9 + 4 - 2
2. Calculate: 7 * 4 - 5 * 2

Solutions:

1. 8
2. 18

Operations with fractions and decimals

3. Simplify: 5/8 + 3/4
4. Calculate: 2.5 - 1.3

Solutions:

3. 11/8 or 1 3/8

4. 1.2

Ratios, proportions, and percentages

5. If 4/x = 6/9, find x

6. Calculate 15% of 120

Solutions:

5. x = 6

6. 18

Powers and square roots

7. Calculate: 2^3

8. Find the square root of 64

Solutions:

7. 8

8. 8

Least common multiple and greatest common divisor

9. Find the LCM of 4 and 6

10. Find the GCD of 8 and 12

Solutions:

9. 12

10. 4

Algebraic expressions

11. Simplify: 3(2x + 4) - x

12. Simplify: 4a - 2(a - 3)

Solutions:

11. 5x + 12

12. 2a + 6

Linear equations of one variable

13. Solve: $4x + 7 = 19$

14. Solve: $5y - 9 = 11$

Solutions:

13. $x = 3$

14. $y = 4$

Linear inequalities of one variable

15. Solve: $3x - 5 > 4$

16. Solve: $2z + 1 < 7$

Solutions:

15. $x > 3$

16. $z < 3$

Systems of linear equations

17. Solve the system: $2x + y = 5 \quad x - y = 1$

18. Solve the system: $3a + 2b = 7 \quad a - b = 1$

Solutions:

17. $x = 2, y = 1$

18. $a = 3, b = 2$

Properties of numbers (associative, commutative, distributive)

19. Verify the commutative property of the sum for $4 + 5$

20. Check the distributive property for $3(x + 4)$

Solutions:

19. $5 + 4 = 9$

20. $3x + 12$

Mini Test: Pre-Algebra and Elementary Algebra

1. Simplify: $18 - 4 + 2 - 7$

2. Calculate: $8 * 5 - 3 * 2$

3. Simplify: $7/9 + 1/3$

4. Calculate: 3.4 - 1.7

5. If 5/y = 10/15, find y

6. Calculate 20% of 150

7. Calculate: 3^4

8. Find the square root of 81

9. Find the LCM of 6 and 8

10. Find the GCD of 9 and 12

11. Simplify: 2(3x - 2) + 4x

12. Simplify: 5a - 3(a - 2)

13. Solve: 3x + 5 = 20

14. Solve: 6y - 8 = 16

15. Solve: 2x - 3 > 5

16. Solve: 4z + 2 < 10

17. Solve the system: 2x + 3y = 13 x - y = 1

18. Solve the system: 4a + b = 9 2a - b = 1

19. Check the associative property of addition for: (3 + 4) + 5

20. Check the distributive property for 2(2x + 5)

Mini test answers

1. 9

2. 34

3. 10/9 or 1 1/9

4. 1.7

5. y = 7.5

6. 30

7. 81

8. 9

9. 24

10. 3

11. 10x - 4

12. 2a + 6

13. x = 5

14. y = 4

15. x > 4

16. z < 2

17. x = 4, y = 3

18. a = 2, b = 1

19. 3 + (4 + 5) = 12

20. 4x + 10

Practice Questions: Intermediate Algebra and Coordinate Geometry

Quadratic equations

1. Solve: $x^2 - 5x + 6 = 0$

2. Solve: $2x^2 + 3x - 2 = 0$

Solutions:

1. x = 2, 3

2. x = -2, 1/2

Functions and their graphics

3. Find the value of $f(x) = 3x^2 - 2x + 1$ when x = 2

4. Determine the domain of $f(x) = 1/(x+2)$

Solutions:

3. f (2) = 9

4. All real numbers except (x = -2)

Quadratic inequalities

5. Solve the inequality: $x^2 - 4x - 5 > 0$

6. Solve the inequality: $3x^2 - 2x - 1 < 0$

Solutions:

5. x < -1 or x > 5

6. -1/3 < x < 1

Polynomials and factoring

7. Factor: $x^3 - 3x^2 + 2x$

8. Factor: $4x^2 - 9$

Solutions:

7. $x(x - 1)(x - 2)$

8. $(2x - 3)(2x + 3)$

Rational expressions

9. Simplify: $(x^2 - 9)/(x^2 - 6x + 9)$

10. Simplify: $(2x^2 - 8)/(4x)$

Solutions:

9. $(x + 3)/(x - 3)$

10. $(x - 2)/2$

Exponential and logarithmic equations

11. Solve: $2^x = 8$

12. Solve: $\log(x) + \log(2) = 1$

Solutions:

11. $x = 3$

12. $x = 5$

Systems of nonlinear equations

13. Solve the system: $y = x^2$ $y = 2x + 3$

14. Solve the system: $x^2 + y^2 = 25$ $x - y = 1$

Solutions:

13. $x = 3, y = 9$ or $x = -1, y = 1$

14. $x = 3, y = 2$ or $x = -4, y = -5$

Properties and operations with matrices

15. Find the transpose of the matrix: [[1, 2], [3, 4]]

16. Calculate the determinant of the matrix: [[2, 3], [1, 4]]

Solutions:

15. [[1, 3], [2, 4]]

16. 5

Distance between two points on the plane

17. Calculate the distance between the points (1,2) and (4,6)

18. Find the distance between the points (-3, 5) and (3, 5)

Solutions:

17. 5

18. 6

The slope of a straight line

19. Find the slope of the line that passes through the points (2,3) and (5,7)

20. Calculate the slope of the line that passes through the points (-1, -1) and (2, 3)

Solutions:

19. 4/3

20. 4/3

Equation of the line

21. Write the equation of the line in a point-slope form that passes through (2,3) with slope 2

22. Write the equation of the line in slope-intercept form with slope 3 and passing through the point (1,2)

Solutions:

21. $y - 3 = 2(x - 2)$

22. $y = 3x - 1$

Geometric transformations (translation, reflection, rotation, dilation)

23. Describe the transformation: $f(x) = (x - 3)^2 + 2$

24. Describe the transformation: $g(x) = -2(x + 1)^2 + 4$

Solutions:

23. Translation 3 units to the right and 2 units up

24. Reflection on the x-axis, vertical dilation by a factor of 2, translation 1 unit to the left and 4 units up

Mini Test: Intermediate Algebra and Coordinate Geometry

1. Solve: $x^2 + 2x - 8 = 0$

2. Solve: $3x^2 - 5x + 2 = 0$

3. Find the value of $f(x) = x^3 - x + 1$ when $x = -1$

4. Determine the domain of $f(x) = sqrt(x-1)$

5. Solve the inequality: $x^2 - 2x - 3 > 0$

6. Solve the inequality: $x^2 + 4x + 3 < 0$

7. Factor: $x^3 - x^2 - 4x + 4$

8. Factor: $9x^2 - 16$

9. Simplify: $(x^2 - 4x + 4)/ (x^2 - 4)$

10. Simplify: $(3x^2 - 6)/(6x)$

11. Solve: $3^x = 27$

12. Solve: $log(x+1) - log(x-1) = 1$

13. Solve the system: $y = x^2 + 1$ $y = 3x + 2$

14. Find the transpose of the matrix: $[[1, 0], [2, 3]]$

15. Calculate the distance between the points $(0,0)$ and $(5,12)$

16. Find the slope of the line that passes through the points $(1,2)$ and $(3,6)$

17. Write the equation of the line in a point-slope form that passes through $(1,1)$ with slope -2

18. Describe the transformation: $h(x) = -x^2 + 3$

Mini test answers

1. $x = -4, 2$

2. $x = 1, 2/3$

3. $f(-1) = 1$

4. $x >= 1$

103

5. x < -1 or x > 3

6. -3 < x < -1

7. (x^2 - 4) (x - 1)

8. (3x - 4) (3x + 4)

9. (x - 2)/ (x + 2)

10. x/2

11. x = 3

12. x = 10

13. x = -1, y = 0 or x = 1, y = 4

14. [[1, 2], [0, 3]]

15. 13

16. 2

17. y - 1 = -2(x - 1)

18. Reflection on the x-axis and translation 3 units upward

Practice Questions: Plane Geometry and Trigonometry
Angles and their measurements

1. Convert 60 degrees to radians.

2. Convert pi/4 radians to degrees.

Solutions:

1. pi/3 radians

2. 45 degrees

Properties of triangles (isosceles, equilateral, right angles)

3. Find the length of the hypotenuse of a right triangle with legs of 6 and 8 units.

4. Find the measure of each angle in an equilateral triangle.

Solutions:

3. 10 units

4. 60 degrees

Relationships in right triangles (Pythagorean theorem)

5. Calculate the length of the missing leg in a right triangle with a 13-unit hypotenuse and a 5-unit leg.

6. Determine if a triangle with sides of 9, 12, and 15 units is a right angle.

Solutions:

5. 12 units

6. Yes, it is a right triangle.

Properties of circles

7. Calculate the area of a circle with a radius of 4 units.

8. Find the circumference of a circle with a diameter of 14 units.

Solutions:

7. 16pi square units

8. 14pi units

Relationships between angles and arcs of a circle

9. Find the measurement of the arc in a circle with a radius of 5 units and a central angle of 72 degrees.

10. Determine the length of the arc corresponding to a central angle of 120 degrees in a circle with a radius of 7 units.

Solutions:

9. 2pi units

10. 14pi/3 units

Areas and perimeters of polygons

11. Calculate the area of a triangle with a base of 8 units and a height of 5 units.

12. Find the perimeter of a regular pentagon with sides of 6 units.

Solutions:

11. 20 square units

12. 30 units

Volumes and surface areas of solids

13. Calculate the volume of a cylinder with a radius of 4 units and a height of 9 units.

14. Find the surface area of a sphere with a radius of 5 units.

Solutions:

13. 144pi cubic units

14. 100pi square units

Fundamental trigonometric identities

15. Simplify the expression: $\sin^2(x) + \cos^2(x)$.

16. Express $\tan(x)$ in terms of $\sin(x)$ and $\cos(x)$.

Solutions:

15. 1

16. $\sin(x)/\cos(x)$

Trigonometric functions and their graphs

17. Find the value of $\sin(\pi/3)$.

18. Determine the value of $\cos(30\text{ degrees})$.

Solutions:

17. $\sqrt{3}/2$

18. $\sqrt{3}/2$

Law of sines and cosines

19. Use the law of sines to find the angle opposite a side of 7 units in a triangle with sides of 7, 9, and 12 units. (Assume the angle opposite the 9-unit side is 60 degrees.)

20. Use the law of cosines to find the third side of a triangle with sides of 5 and 7 units and an included angle of 45 degrees.

Solutions:

19. 48.59 degrees

20. $\sqrt{34 - 35\cos(45\text{ degrees})}$

Applications of trigonometry to real-life problems

21. Calculate the height of a tree that casts a shadow of 15 units with an angle of elevation to the sun of 30 degrees.

22. Find the distance a ship sees a lighthouse with an elevation angle of 30 degrees from a height of 20 units.

Solutions:

21. 15sqrt (3) units

22. 20sqrt (3) units

Mini Test: Plane Geometry and Trigonometry

1. Convert 45 degrees to radians.

2. Find the length of the missing leg in a right triangle with a 17-unit hypotenuse and an 8-unit leg.

3. Calculate the area of a triangle with sides of 6, 8, and 10 units.

4. Find the length of the arc corresponding to a central angle of 90 degrees in a circle with a radius of 5 units.

5. Calculate the area of a regular polygon with 8 sides of length 3 units.

6. Determine the volume of a cone with a radius of 3 units and a height of 7 units.

7. Use the fundamental trigonometric identity to simplify $\sin^2(x) + \cos^2(x)$.

8. Find the value of tan (pi/4).

9. Use the law of sines to find an angle in a triangle with sides of 5, 12, and 13 units (assume the angle opposite the 12-unit side is 90 degrees).

10. Calculate the distance of an object at a height of 12 units when viewed at an elevation angle of 60 degrees.

Mini exam answers

1. pi/4 radians

2. 15 units

3. 24 square units

4. 5pi/2 units

5. 54 square units

6. 21pi cubic units

7. 1

8. 1

9. 22.62 degrees

10. 12sqrt (3) units

Chapter 7: Scientific Reasoning

Scientific reasoning focuses on evaluating analytical and reasoning skills rather than specific scientific knowledge. You do not need to be a science expert, just be able to interpret, analyze, and reason with the information presented to you.

The first thing you'll notice is a variety of graphs, tables, and experiment descriptions. The core skill being tested is your ability to read and interpret them. So, if you are looking at a graph that shows how the temperature varies throughout the day. Your task is not to recite the laws of thermodynamics. It is to observe how temperature changes and be able to describe that modification. You should ask yourself what patterns you see, what stands out, and how they relate to the information given.

You should be prepared to make logical connections between different pieces of information. If a passage mentions concentration improves with classical music but worsens with noisy background music, you should be able to deduce why these results might be valid and what factors might influence them.

The attitude with which you must face this section is one of curiosity and calm. Don't be intimidated by technical or complex terms. If you come across a question that seems complicated, take a moment to break it down, look for the parts you understand, and build your answer from there.

Next, I present the theoretical content you should review. At the end of the theoretical segments, you will find one with practical questions and analysis:

Representation of Data, Research Summaries, and Conflicting Criteria

Keep these theoretical aspects in mind:

Reading Bar, Line, and Pie Charts

Bar graphs allow you to compare content between different categories using bars of different heights or lengths. To interpret them, take into account the categories on the horizontal axis and the values on the vertical axis. Observe the height of each bar to compare the values represented. If you find a bar higher than the others, it represents a greater value. Read the labels and legends to understand what each bar represents and verify the units of measurement.

Line graphs aim to observe how they change. Follow the line from left to right and analyze the points where it rises, falls, or remains stable; these changes in direction indicate variations in the trend. An ascending line indicates an increase in values, while a descending one indicates a decrease. The values on the axes help you understand the magnitude of these changes.

Pie charts show the proportion of each part concerning the total. Each segment represents a percentage of the whole circle. To interpret them, examine the size of each segment in comparison to the entire circle. Compare the largest and smallest segments to determine which categories have the largest and smallest proportions.

Interpretation of Circular Tables

These present information in the form of percentages or fractions that add up to a total. To interpret them, place the main categories and their subcategories, and look at the numerical values and their labels to understand what percentage of the total each data represents. If one shows the distribution of a company's budget, each category such as marketing, development, and operations will have a value-associated percentage.

If marketing has 30% of the total budget, this is the largest segment and therefore represents the majority of the purchase.

Practice adding the percentages to verify that the individual values add up to the correct total.

Analysis of Diagrams and Circular Schemes

Unlike bar, line, and pie charts, which represent quantitative data, these show how different components of a system are interconnected.

To analyze them, place each element and its function within the diagram, and look at the arrows and lines that connect the elements. These indicate the flow of information or a process. If it shows the water cycle, you will see stages such as evaporation, condensation, and precipitation connected by arrows indicating the movement of water through each phase.

Pay attention to the legends, as they give details about each component. On the test, you might find a circular diagram that illustrates the operation of a power plant. You will need to look at each part of the diagram, such as the boiler, turbine, and generator, and then follow the connections showing how the energy flows through the system, and the directions of the arrows to understand how energy is transformed at each stage.

To practice, take diagrams from books or online resources and try to locate all the components and their interconnection without reading the accompanying explanation.

Comparison and Contrast

On the ACT, approach this task by reading the question to understand what aspects you need to compare, and then review the graphs, tables, or text.

For the comparison process, look for similar or different values. If you have two bars showing monthly sales for two different years, note which months have similar sales and which show significant variation. Keep a mental record of these months and use this information to answer. If they show sales in millions, compare the same values.

Contrasting requires locating key differences. If two tables are presented with information on the population of different cities, review each category (such as population density or growth rate) and find the discrepancies. In this case, one city could have a higher population density but a lower growth rate compared to another. These observations will help you answer specific differences between the data sets.

Trends and Patterns

These reveal behaviors and changes. A trend is a general direction in which the data appears to move. An ascending one shows a constant increase in values, while a descending one indicates a decrease. A pattern is a repetition or a consistent relationship noted.

Let's say you are faced with a line graph on the exam showing the monthly average temperature over several years. Look at the line and follow it from left to right. If it goes up from January to July and then goes down from July to December, you are faced with a seasonal trend, where the temperature increases in the summer months and decreases in the winter months.

Look for keys, like peaks and valleys. These are where the trend changes. Next, look at the general direction. If you see a repeating pattern, such as seasonal fluctuations, make a mental note of these repeats.

Understanding Independent and Dependent Variables

The independent is the one manipulated or changed to observe its effect, while the dependent is the one measured or observed to see how it responds to changes in the independent.

In a study on plant growth, the amount of water given is independent, since it can be controlled and adjusted. Growth, measured in height, is dependent because it is observed how it changes in response to the amount of water.

Evaluation of the Methodology and Conclusions

To evaluate the methodology, look at the design, how samples were selected, how groups were assigned, and what variables were controlled.

Let's say you have a description of the effect of light on plant growth. Note if you have a control group and an experimental group.

See if the steps are clear and replicable. If it mentions those were watered "regularly" without specifying the exact amount of water, it could be a weakness in the methodology. The lack of precise details affects reliability.

Review how they were collected and whether a measurement method was used. If it is inconsistent it will lead to incorrect conclusions. If research on the effect of a new drug does not use a placebo, it could be questionable.

Recognition of Conflicting Criteria in Scientific Texts

On the test you might be faced with two passages discussing the same topic, such as the impact of climate change on the oceans, but with different opinions.

Read each one and underline the key claims and evidence presented. One author might say rising water temperatures are causing fish populations to decline, while another might attribute it to overfishing.

Comparing the evidence used by each author will help you see the bases. If one cites recent, specific studies while the other relies on older or less detailed data, it will influence credibility. Analyze whether the evidence is relevant and sufficient to support each criterion.

Maintain a critical and objective reading, and practice with different ones to relate to this type of analysis.

Critical Analysis of Arguments and Evidence

Look for what claim the author is making and what evidence they give to support it. Look for any unsupported assumptions or overgeneralizations. If you claim that all students perform better on tests after listening to classical music without citing specific studies, this is an unsubstantiated assumption.

Examine the quality of the evidence, whether it is accurate or whether citations of reliable statistics strengthen an argument. If it mentions a study, check whether the results are interpreted correctly and if it is relevant.

Do not rush to accept the content at face value. Be critical and look for inconsistencies or weaknesses in the argument.

Using Visual Information to Support Conclusions

Visual information on the ACT could include graphs, charts, and diagrams; these elements support the conclusions in the passages. To use this information effectively, look at the type of table being presented, and find the axes, labels, and legend to understand what is being displayed.

When faced with a question requiring interpreting visual content, review the graph before reading it in full. If you see a graph of bars comparing the growth rates of different plants under different light conditions, look at which bar represents each condition and its values.

If it mentions a specific condition that results in increased growth, check to see if this matches.

Interpretation of Experiments and Scientific Information

These are the elements that will allow you to interpret correctly:

Hypotheses and Objectives

A hypothesis predicts a relationship between variables and can be tested. Objectives specify what is sought to be discovered or confirmed.

For a hypothesis, look for a statement indicating an assumption or prediction. This statement will appear early in the passage and will suggest a relationship intended to be proven.

In a study on the effect of temperature on physical activity, it could be that "people perform less physical activity at extreme temperatures." This statement predicts a direct relationship.

For objectives, look for statements explaining what is being measured and why. They are detailed after the hypothesis and describe the specific variables that will be examined and evaluated. They might include measuring the amount of physical activity at different temperatures and determining the impact of extreme temperatures. Phrases like "this study aims to..." or "it is expected that..." clarify the goals and provide a framework for interpretation.

Understanding of Procedures and Designs

Procedures are specific steps, while design is the general structure guiding development.

To understand procedures, look for detailed descriptions of stages. Note how variables are manipulated; if investigating academic performance under different lighting conditions, procedures might detail how lighting conditions are set and academic performance measured. Pay attention to any protocol variations, as inconsistencies affect reliability.

Design includes aspects such as participant selection, group assignments, and the use of controls. it should control influencing variables. For instance, studying the impact of an exercise program on cardiovascular health requires verifying that comparison groups are similar in age, gender, and initial health status. This is achieved through random assignment and use of control groups. To understand this, examine how the study was structured, participant selection, group division, and measures ensuring group equivalence. Note mentions of randomization or blind group use.

By understanding these elements, you can better evaluate the quality and ability to answer research questions.

Analysis of Results

Imagine research measuring the reaction rate of different chemicals at varying temperatures. Review collected values per temperature, noting patterns like faster reactions at higher temperatures, supporting the initial hypothesis.

Examine the means and variations. If the chemical reaction occurs faster at 122°F than at 86°F, it indicates temperature affects the reaction rate. Evaluate whether the differences are consistent, suggesting temperature (independent) influences reaction speed (dependent).

Take into account possible errors that could have affected results. If unexpected variability appears, check if all relevant variables were controlled, such as substance purity or instrument precision.

Look for trends and patterns; for example, whether all chemical reactions, regardless of substance type, accelerate with increasing temperature. Identifying such patterns confirms support for the hypothesis and investigates a direct relationship between manipulated variables and observed results.

If the methods used align with hypothesis expectations, it was likely well-designed.

Evaluation of Controls and Variables

Imagine research measuring the effect of different pH levels on organic matter decomposition pH (independent variable) affects the decomposition rate (dependent variable).

Examine how the other variables that could influence have been controlled and see if all the organic matter samples were exposed to the same environmental conditions, such as temperature and humidity.

See if there is a sample that has not been treated with the different pH levels, to compare and determine if the changes are due to the manipulation of the independent variable. This comparison allows validation of the effect of pH on decomposition.

See if a sufficient number of samples were used and if they were replicated. A large sample size and replication of the trials increase reliability and allow more robust conclusions to be drawn.

Evaluate researcher expectations influencing data collection or interpretation. Unacknowledged biases compromise validity.

Results Comparison

Examine the methods used in each experiment, analyzing whether the procedures were similar and whether the conditions were kept constant. If one measures reaction time at different noise levels and another evaluates reaction time at different light intensities, analyze whether the methods for measuring reaction time were consistent to verify that the comparisons are valid.

Check if the results of both are expressed in the same units of measurement and if the data are presented similarly. If these are in different formats, convert them to a common unit for a direct comparison.

Take into account sample sizes and variability. A larger sample size and lower variability increase confidence. If one has a small sample and the other a large sample, consider how this affects reliability.

Assess conclusions for support and acknowledgment of limitations. Differing conclusions like noise increasing reaction time vs. light's no effect question analyzed variables or design errors.

Recognition of Errors and Biases

Examine the study design, including control group presence. Absent controls introduce bias, making results unreliable. In advertising's impact on consumer behavior, no unexposed group prevents attributing changes to the independent variable.

Review how subjects were selected and assigned; see if the selection was random, and if subjects were assigned to groups in a way that minimized pre-existing differences. The lack of randomization means that they reflect differences between the groups rather than the effect of the independent variable.

Find out if reliable measurement instruments were used and if the procedures were consistent for all subjects. Consider sample size and replication. Evaluate potential researcher bias, acknowledging or mitigating it to enhance validity.

Integration of Information from Multiple Sources to Formulate Conclusions

For this, you must find the different sources available: graphics, tables, descriptions, and explanatory texts. Understand the purpose of each and how it relates to the overall objective.

Read each one separately and write down the keys; see what information each one gives and how it is connected to the hypothesis or objective. If you find a graph showing the number of hours of study and the scores obtained in a test, and another discussing the techniques, connect them to see how they complement each other. The correlation between more hours and better scores could be supported by the explanation of effective techniques.

Check if the results match the observations or statements made; if one graph shows an increase in response accuracy with practice and another describes how practice improves memory, integrating this data strengthens your conclusion.

Analyze discrepancies, understanding their impact on validity. Synthesize all sources, clearly expressing conclusions based on combined evidence.

Practice and Analysis Questions

Data Representation

Analysis of a bar chart

Imagine a bar graph showing the average hours of sleep of college students during an exam week and a normal week. On the graph, the horizontal axis represents the days of the week (Monday to Sunday), and the vertical axis shows the average hours of sleep (0 to 10 hours). There are two bars for each day, one for exam week and one for normal week:

- What day of the week has the greatest difference in average hours of sleep between exam week and normal week?

- Analyze why this difference could exist and how it affects students' academic performance.

Analysis: To answer this question, view the bars on the graph. The greatest difference in average sleep hours will be seen as the greater space between the heights of the two bars on the same day. Suppose Monday shows a big difference, with the exam week bar being much lower than the normal week bar. This suggests students sleep less at the beginning of exam week, affecting concentration, memory, and academic performance.

Interpreting a line chart

View a line graph showing the number of visitors to a national park during a year. The horizontal axis represents the months of the year, and the vertical axis indicates the number of visitors (in thousands). The line moves up and down reflecting the variability in the number of visitors month to month:

- During which month was the maximum peak of visitors observed?

- Suggest possible factors that could explain the increase in visitors that month.

Analysis: To identify the maximum peak, imagine the line on the chart reaching its highest point in a specific month. Let's assume the peak is in July. This month coincides with the summer holidays, a more favorable climate for special events in the park that attract more visitors. The identification of these factors serves to understand variations in the number of visitors.

Evaluating a pie chart

Imagine a pie chart showing the distribution of a company's annual budget across different departments. The segments of the graph represent Research and Development, Marketing, Sales, Operations and Human Resources:

- Which department receives the most of the budget and which receives the least?

- Evaluate how this distribution reflects the company's strategic priorities.

Analysis: View the pie chart and observe the sizes of the segments. The largest segment, Research and Development, receives the majority of the budget, while the smallest, Human Resources, receives the least. This distribution suggests the company prioritizes innovation and the development of new products or services, while personnel management could have a lower priority in terms of investment. Understanding how the budget is distributed helps interpret the company's objectives.

Research Summaries

Identification of hypotheses and objectives

Read the following research summary:

"A recent study investigated the impact of regular physical activity on the mental health of older adults. The researchers proposed that regular exercise improves psychological well-being. The objective was to compare stress and anxiety levels in older adults who exercise regularly with those who lead a sedentary lifestyle."

- Identify the hypothesis.

116

- What are the specific objectives of this research?

Analysis: The hypothesis is regular exercise improves the psychological well-being of older adults. Specific objectives include comparing stress and anxiety levels between two groups of older adults: those who exercise regularly and those who do not. To identify this in a passage, look for statements that predict a relationship between variables and statements describing what will be measured and how it will be evaluated.

Evaluation of results

The results are presented:

"The results showed older adults who exercised reported lower levels of stress and anxiety compared to those who did not. Additionally, participants who exercised showed greater satisfaction with their quality of life."

- Do the results support the initial hypothesis? Explain your reasoning.

- What conclusions are drawn from these results?

Analysis: They do support the initial hypothesis since they indicate regular exercise is associated with lower levels of stress and anxiety, as well as greater satisfaction with quality of life. Conclusions could include that encouraging physical activity in older adults is an effective strategy to improve their mental health and general well-being.

Critical analysis of the methodology

Read the description of the method used:

"The participants were randomly selected and divided into two groups: one did regular physical exercise and the other did not. A validated questionnaire was used to measure stress and anxiety levels, and monthly follow-ups were done for a year."

- Evaluate the validity of the method used.

- What improvements or additional controls could be implemented to increase the reliability of the results?

Analysis: Validity appears adequate given the use of random selection and the use of a validated questionnaire. However, improvements could be implemented such as using additional objective measures (such as stress biomarkers), considering other influencing factors (such as diet or social support), and including follow-up to observe sustained effects.

Conflicting Criteria

Comparison of arguments

Read the following criteria about the use of technology in education:

Criterion A: "The use of technology in the classroom improves student participation and performance. Digital tools allow greater personalization of learning and facilitate access to a wide range of educational resources."

Criterion B: "The excessive use of technology in the classroom distracts students and reduces their ability to concentrate. In addition, dependence on electronic devices limits the development of social skills and critical thinking."

- Compare the arguments presented in both criteria.

- What evidence could you look for to support or refute each of these arguments?

Analysis: Criterion A emphasizes the benefits of technology, such as personalization of learning and access to resources. Criterion B highlights possible disadvantages, such as distraction and limitations in the development of social skills. Evidence to support or refute these arguments could include empirical studies on the impact of technology on academic performance, direct observation of classroom behavior, and surveys of student and teacher satisfaction and perceptions.

Evaluation of contradictory evidence

Read the following summaries about the impact of remote work:

#1: "Found that employees who work remotely report higher levels of job satisfaction and lower stress due to schedule flexibility and the elimination of commute time."

#2: "Another indicated that remote work leads to a sense of social isolation and less team cohesion, which impacts employee productivity and emotional well-being."

- Discuss how both offer a comprehensive view of the impact of remote work.

- How could you integrate the results to formulate a balanced conclusion?

Analysis: Both present positive and negative aspects of remote work. The first highlights the benefits in terms of flexibility and stress reduction, while the second points out problems such as social isolation and team cohesion. To formulate a balanced conclusion, you could consider that remote work offers significant advantages but requires strategies to mitigate its disadvantages, such as encouraging communication and teamwork.

Analysis of opposing perspectives

Consider the following opinions about the impact of social media on interpersonal communication:

Opinion A: "Social networks have revolutionized communication, allowing people to connect and share experiences with a global audience, which enriches interpersonal relationships."

Opinion B: "Excessive use of social media damages personal relationships, creating an illusion of connection while diminishing the quality and depth of face-to-face interactions."

- Describe how you could design a study to evaluate these conflicting opinions.

- What type of data and methodology would be necessary to obtain reliable results?

Analysis: To evaluate these opinions, you could design a longitudinal study measuring the quality of interpersonal relationships and social media use in a diverse sample of participants. You could use questionnaires to assess satisfaction and depth of interactions, along with records of the type of social media usage

Part III:

Mastering the Writing Test

Chapter 8: Writing With Purpose

To write your essay you can use some of the grammar and spelling tips I shared in chapter four, although I presented them to you in preparation for the English section.

Therefore, I will now present some more aspects related to this step:

Understand the Writing Prompt

Keep these keys in mind for a better understanding:

Read the Instructions

Read it carefully when you receive it. Do not rush, and look at each word and phrase carefully, to detect the verbs used, such as "analyze", "describe" or "compare", since they indicate the approach you should take.

Do not overlook the specific details. The keywords will guide you toward the precise aspects you must address. By breaking them down you will be able to have a clear vision of what is expected of you, preventing you from deviating from the central topic.

Determine the Main Theme

This is the core, the central idea, which will guide you. Look at the specific questions or statements. What is it about? What specific aspect do they want you to explore or analyze?

Sometimes, the topic could be explicit, but other times it will require a deeper interpretation. Think about the implications to identify the main topic in which controversy or situation you must address. Always keep the main topic in mind throughout the writing process.

Recognize the Purpose

To define it, look at the prompt and look for clues that tell you whether you should persuade, explain, or analyze a topic. Think about the main objective you hope to achieve with your writing. If it asks you to compare two theories, the purpose is to analyze the differences and similarities, and you might come to a conclusion about which one is more effective.

If you are asked to argue for or against a position, your goal will be to convince the reader using solid evidence and reasoning. This purpose could also be educational, where you need to inform and clarify complex concepts to the reader. The important point is to determine this, because only then will you be able to focus your research well.

Identify the Audience

The audience influences how you should present and what type of language you use. If it is aimed at experts in a specific field, use technical terminology and assume prior knowledge of the topic. On the other hand, if it is general, you will need to explain concepts and avoid complex jargon.

Think about your readers' interests, values, and expectations. What type of information are they looking for? An essay aimed at high school students should be clear, direct, and educational, giving concrete examples and detailed explanations.

Taking into account the context in which it will be read, an academic one will require a more formal and structured treatment; but an opinion article in a newspaper allows for a more personal and direct style.

Note Any Specific Restrictions or Requirements

Taking note of any specific restrictions or requirements is necessary to meet the evaluator's expectations.

These restrictions could include word limits, specific formats, allowed font types, or required structures. Ignoring these details will result in a loss in grade, even if the content is excellent.

If you are asked for a 500-word essay and you turn in a 700-word essay, you could be penalized for not following the instructions. Some will require a particular style, such as MLA or APA, and adhering to these standards shows your attention to detail and your ability to follow academic guidelines. You may find specific requirements about your approach to the topic, such as discussing certain aspects in detail or avoiding others. These restrictions guide your research and help you focus on what is most relevant.

Planning and Organization of the Test

Now you have clarity regarding the instructions, proceed to plan and organize:

Brainstorm

This process serves to explore a wide range of thoughts without restrictions, helping you discover angles and approaches that you may not have considered.

Grab a piece of paper and a pen, or use a digital tool, and write down any ideas that come to mind related to the topic of your essay. Don't worry about quality or relevance at this early stage; the goal is to unleash your creativity and explore all the possibilities.

After a few minutes, review your notes and begin to decide which ones seem most promising and aligned with the brief, which ones have the most potential to be developed in-depth, and which ones could support your main thesis.

Create a Basic Outline or Structure

Developing an outline or basic structure gives it shape and coherence. Starting from the thesis, build the basic structure around it. Visualize it as a series of interconnected blocks. Start with an introduction presenting the topic and capture the reader's attention, culminating in your main thesis.

Each paragraph should begin with a topic sentence stating its purpose, followed by evidence and analysis; transitions are necessary to maintain fluidity and coherence, guiding the reader from one to the next without abrupt interruptions.

This outline will serve as a map to guide your writing, allowing you to focus on developing in an orderly and logical manner. Don't worry, in the following tips I will present them to you in more detail.

Identify Support Points

They are the pillars on which your essay is built. They represent the main ideas and help to develop it coherently and persuasively.

To establish them, ask yourself what statements you could make that convincingly support it. Each one should be relevant and related, provide evidence, and organize them in a logical order that facilitates the reader's understanding.

You could opt for a chronological, cause and effect, or another sequence, depending on which is most appropriate for your topic. Each point should be introduced and developed in a separate paragraph, beginning with a clear topic sentence indicating the main idea of the paragraph, and should be well developed, using data, quotes, and analysis.

Establish a Clear Introduction

The introduction of an essay is essential for capturing the reader's attention and setting the tone.

Start with a powerful sentence to pique the interest. Whether it is provocative, a surprising statistic, or a quote, it should draw the reader in and motivate them to continue reading.

After capturing attention, provide context that helps place your topic in a broader framework, explaining why it is relevant. It should be clear and concise enough for the reader to understand. Next, present the central idea; it should be specific and debatable, offering clear direction.

Plan Development Paragraphs

To create an effective development, plan each paragraph. Start with a clear topic sentence; it should be specific, and then present evidence such as relevant quotes, data, or anecdotes.

Each piece should be well explained and analyzed and use smooth transitions to connect each sentence so the reader can follow your line of thought effortlessly.

Define a Solid Conclusion

Summarize as briefly as possible the key points you have discussed in the development. It should be concise and not introduce new information. Reaffirm your thesis in a way reflecting the depth and progress.

It should offer a sense of closure and come full circle, with an emotional and reflective impact, connecting the topic to a broader context, and showing the relevance and implications of your argument.

Include a call to action or a final reflection inviting you to think further.

Writing, Reviewing, and Editing Techniques

With these techniques, you can polish your essay:

Write the First Draft Without Worrying About Perfection

When writing it, focus on expressing your thoughts fluently, without stopping to correct every mistake or polish every sentence. This way you can maintain the creative momentum and avoid blockages arising from worrying too much about accuracy. Do it as if it were a conversation with yourself, where you explore your ideas.

Don't be afraid to make mistakes; these are part of the process and give you a clearer vision of how to develop it.

Write with honesty and passion, knowing you will have the opportunity to review and improve your work later.

Review Clarity and Consistency

To achieve clarity, use direct and simple language, avoiding unnecessary jargon or complicated phrases. When reviewing your work, read each paragraph and verify each one develops a single main idea. If the reader follows your line of thought without getting lost, you are doing well. So read what you have written; do it out loud, so you can detect confusing phrases or grammatical structures needing adjustments, and check each idea connects naturally with the next, creating a flow of information that is easy to follow. Coherence is achieved by seeing each section relates to your thesis and that the conclusions are logical and well-founded.

Check the Relevance and Strength of the Evidence and the Transition

Examine each piece of information, quote, or example and see if it strengthens your argument. It must be accurate and come from reliable sources, avoiding generalizations and unfounded assumptions. It must be explained and connected to what you are doing.

The transition between paragraphs is necessary to maintain coherence and flow. A good transition guides the reader from one idea to another without abrupt interruptions, creating a natural flow. They can be subtle but effective, such as indicating a cause-and-effect relationship, contrasting, or adding additional information.

These transitions improve readability, strengthening cohesion, and showing how each point fits into a broader, more persuasive whole.

Check Grammar, Spelling, and Unnecessary Repetitions

These technical aspects could affect the clarity of your message and the reader's perception of your professionalism and attention to detail. In this review, verify that each sentence follows the correct grammatical rules. Pay attention to subject-verb agreement, proper verb tense usage, and correct sentence construction. Use grammar-checking tools, but also trust your own judgment and understanding of the language.

Spelling errors distract the reader and diminish the credibility of your work. Check each word and use a spell checker to catch errors that might have gone unnoticed.

Unnecessary repetitions make your essay seem redundant and unprofessional. Look for words and phrases that are repeated unnecessarily. Replace them with synonyms or rephrase sentences to avoid monotony.

Part IV:
Practice Makes Perfect

Chapter 9: Complete Practice Exams

When you take the ACT under timed conditions, you are preparing yourself for real pressure. Sitting with a stopwatch allows you to adapt to the limited time you will have and feel the urgency.

So, when you practice, replicate the conditions of the exam. Sit in a quiet place, use a stopwatch, and avoid interruptions. The more you practice this way, the more comfortable you will feel and the better prepared you will be to take on the ACT.

ACT 1 Simulation Test

Section 1: English (75 Questions in 45 minutes)

Passage 1: Jane Austen was born in 1775 and grew up in a family that loved literature. Her novels, often featuring strong female characters, were well-received by her contemporaries. Austen's keen observations of human nature and her social commentary have made her works timeless classics. Pride and Prejudice, one of her most famous novels, continues to captivate readers with its wit and insight.

1. Jane Austen was born in 1775 and grew up in a family that loved literature.

   - A) NO CHANGE
   - B) had grown up
   - C) grows up
   - D) have grown up

2. Her novels, often featuring strong female characters, were well-received by her contemporaries.

   - A) NO CHANGE
   - B) were well-received
   - C) is well-received
   - D) has been well-received

3. Austen's keen observations of human nature and her social commentary has made her works timeless classics.

   - A) NO CHANGE
   - B) had made
   - C) have made
   - D) have you made

4. Pride and Prejudice, one of her most famous novels, continues to captivate readers with its wit and insight.

   - A) NO CHANGE
   - B) continue to captivate
   - C) you have continued to captivate
   - D) continues captivating

Passage 2: Climate change is a significant issue that affects many aspects of the environment. Scientists have been studying the impact of climate change for decades, and they continue to find new evidence. The data collected from these studies are used to develop models predicting future climate scenarios. These models help policymakers make informed decisions about how to mitigate the effects of climate change.

5. Climate change is a significant issue that affects many aspects of the environment.

- A) NO CHANGE

- B) are a significant issue

- C) were a significant issue

- D) is a significant issue

6. Scientists have been studying the impact of climate change for decades, and they continue to find new evidence.

- A) NO CHANGE

- B) continued

- C) continue

- D) have continued

7. The data collected from these studies are used to develop models that predict future climate scenarios.

- A) NO CHANGE

- B) is used

- C) were used

- D) has been used

8. These models help policymakers make informed decisions about how to mitigate the effects of climate change.

- A) NO CHANGE

- B) helps

- C) helped

- D) have helped

Passage 3: The invention of the steam engine led to significant changes in industry, including increased production and efficiency. Factories began to produce goods at a much faster rate than they had previously been able to do. This period saw the rise of mass production and the growth of cities as people moved to urban areas for work. Working conditions in factories were often harsh, with long hours and low wages.

9. The invention of the steam engine led to significant changes in industry, including increased production and efficiency.

   - A) NO CHANGE

   - B) leading

   - C) leads to

   - D) has led to

10. Factories began to produce goods at a much faster rate than they had previously been able to do.

    - A) NO CHANGE

    - B) than they did

    - C) than they were

    - D) than they have

11. This period saw the rise of mass production and the growth of cities as people moved to urban areas for work.

    - A) NO CHANGE

    - B) have moved

    - C) moves

    - D) move

12. Working conditions in factories were often harsh, with long hours and low wages.

    - A) NO CHANGE

    - B) they were often harsh

    - C) it was often harsh

    - D) which were often harsh

Passage 4: The group of friends decided to spend their summer vacation hiking through the mountains. They were all experienced hikers, but none of them had ever seen such breathtaking scenery. As they climbed higher, the air became cooler and the views more spectacular. Each night, they set up camp under the stars, sharing stories and enjoying the tranquility.

13. The group of friends decided to spend their summer vacation hiking through the mountains.

    - A) NO CHANGE

    - B) spending

    - C) to spent

    - D) spend

14. They were all experienced hikers, but none of them had ever seen such breathtaking scenery.

    - A) NO CHANGE

    - B) none of them have

    - C) none of them has

    - D) none of them had seen

15. As they climbed higher, the air became cooler and the views more spectacular.

    - A) NO CHANGE

    - B) view's more spectacular

    - C) views were more spectacular

    - D) view more spectacular

16. Each night, they set up camp under the stars, sharing stories and enjoying the tranquility.

    - A) NO CHANGE

    - B) setting up camp

    - C) setting up camp

    - D) seted up camp

Passage 5: Medical technology has advanced rapidly in the past decade, with new treatments and devices improving patient outcomes. One of the most significant developments is the use of robotic surgery, which allows for greater precision and less invasive procedures. Patients who undergo robotic surgery typically experience shorter recovery times and fewer complications. Advances in imaging technology have also made it possible to detect diseases earlier and with greater accuracy.

17. Medical technology has advanced rapidly in the past decade, with new treatments and devices improving patient outcomes.

   - A) NO CHANGE
   - B) in the last decade
   - C) in the past decades
   - D) in the last decades

18. One of the most significant developments is the use of robotic surgery, which allows for greater precision and less invasive procedures.

   - A) NO CHANGE
   - B) which allow
   - C) which allowing
   - D) which allow for

19. Patients who undergo robotic surgery typically experience shorter recovery times and fewer complications.

   - A) NO CHANGE
   - B) experiences
   - C) experiencing
   - D) you have experienced

20. Advances in imaging technology have also made it possible to detect diseases earlier and with greater accuracy.

   - A) NO CHANGE
   - B) have also making
   - C) has also made
   - D) has also making

Passage 6: The city's architecture reflects a blend of various cultural influences, from ancient Roman to medieval Gothic styles. Walking through the narrow streets, one can see buildings that have stood for centuries. The city's central square is surrounded by grand buildings, each with its own unique history. Tourists are often fascinated by the intricate details and craftsmanship of these historic structures.

21. The city's architecture reflects a blend of various cultural influences, from ancient Roman to medieval Gothic styles.

    - A) NO CHANGE

    - B) ancient Roman and medieval Gothic styles

    - C) ancient Roman, and medieval Gothic styles

    - D) ancient Roman; medieval Gothic styles

22. Walking through the narrow streets, one can see buildings that have stood for centuries.

    - A) NO CHANGE

    - B) that stood for centuries.

    - C) that has stood for centuries.

    - D) which standing for centuries.

23. The city's central square is surrounded by grand buildings, each with its own unique history.

    - A) NO CHANGE

    - B) it's own unique history

    - C) its unique history

    - D) its own unique histories

24. Tourists are often fascinated by the intricate details and craftsmanship of these historic structures.

    - A) NO CHANGE

    - B) are fascinated by

    - C) is fascinated by

    - D) were fascinated by

Passage 7: The integration of technology into the classroom has revolutionized the way students learn and teachers teach. With access to digital resources, students can now explore subjects in greater depth and at their own pace. Teachers can use interactive tools to engage students and make learning more dynamic. However, it is important to ensure that technology is used effectively and does not replace fundamental teaching methods.

25. The integration of technology into the classroom has revolutionized the way students learn and teachers teach.

   - A) NO CHANGE

   - B) revolutionized the way students learn, and teachers teach

   - C) revolutionizing the way students learn teachers and teach

   - D) revolutionize the way students learn teachers and teach

26. With access to digital resources, students can now explore subjects in greater depth and at their own pace.

   - A) NO CHANGE

   - B) exploring subjects in greater depth

   - C) explored subjects in greater depth

   - D) explored subjects in greater depth and at their own pace

27. Teachers are able to use interactive tools to engage students and make learning more dynamic.

   - A) NO CHANGE

   - B) is able to use

   - C) is using

   - D) are able use

28. However, it is important to ensure that technology is used effectively and does not replace fundamental teaching methods.

   - A) NO CHANGE

   - B) However it is important to ensure

   - C) However, it is important ensuring

   - D) However it is important ensuring

Passage 8: Biodiversity conservation is essential for maintaining the health of our planet's ecosystems. Different species play unique roles in their environments, contributing to the stability and resilience of ecosystems. Human activities, such as deforestation and pollution, threaten biodiversity and the services that ecosystems provide. Protecting biodiversity is crucial for sustaining the natural processes that support life on Earth.

29. Biodiversity conservation is essential for maintaining the health of our planet's ecosystems.

- A) NO CHANGE

- B) essential to maintain

- C) essential maintaining

- D) essential to maintaining

30. Different species play unique roles in their environments, contributing to the stability and resilience of ecosystems.

- A) NO CHANGE

- B) contributing to the stability and resilience of the ecosystems

- C) contributes to the stability and resilience of ecosystems

- D) contributing to stability and resilience of ecosystems

31. Human activities, such as deforestation and pollution, threaten biodiversity and the services that ecosystems provide.

- A) NO CHANGE

- B) threatened biodiversity

- C) threatening biodiversity

- D) threatens biodiversity

32. Protecting biodiversity is crucial for sustaining the natural processes that support life on Earth.

- A) NO CHANGE

- B) Protecting biodiversity are crucial

- C) Protecting biodiversity has crucial

- D) Protecting biodiversity being crucial

Passage 9: The history of space exploration is filled with remarkable achievements and ongoing challenges. Since the launch of Sputnik 1 in 1957, humans have been fascinated by the possibility of exploring the cosmos. The Apollo moon landings in the 1960s and 1970s represented a significant milestone in space exploration. Today, space agencies around the world continue to pursue ambitious missions to Mars and beyond.

33. The history of space exploration is filled with remarkable achievements and ongoing challenges.

    - A) NO CHANGE

    - B) and ongoing challenging

    - C) and ongoing challenged

    - D) and ongoing challenges

34. Since the launch of Sputnik 1 in 1957, humans have been fascinated by the possibility of exploring the cosmos.

    - A) NO CHANGE

    - B) Since the launch of Sputnik 1 in 1957; humans

    - C) Since the launch of Sputnik 1 in 1957: humans

    - D) Since the launch of Sputnik 1 in 1957 humans,

35. The Apollo moon landings in the 1960s and 1970s represented a significant milestone in space exploration.

    - A) NO CHANGE

    - B) represented significant milestone

    - C) representing a significant milestone

    - D) represents a significant milestone

36. Today, space agencies around the world continue to pursue ambitious missions to Mars and beyond.

    - A) NO CHANGE

    - B) around the world, continue

    - C) around the world; continues

    - D) around the world continues to pursue

Passage 10: Renewable energy sources, such as solar and wind power, are becoming increasingly important as the world seeks to reduce its dependence on fossil fuels. Solar panels convert sunlight into electricity, providing a clean and sustainable energy source. Wind turbines harness the power of the wind to generate electricity without producing harmful emissions. Investing in renewable energy technologies is crucial for achieving a sustainable future.

37. Renewable energy sources, such as solar and wind power, are becoming increasingly important as the world seeks to reduce its dependence on fossil fuels.

   - A) NO CHANGE

   - B) are becoming increasingly important; as the world seeks to reduce its dependence on fossil fuels.

   - C) are becoming increasingly important, as the world seeks to reduce its dependence on fossil fuels.

   - D) are becoming increasingly important as the world seeks to reduce it's dependence on fossil fuels.

38. Solar panels convert sunlight into electricity, providing a clean and sustainable energy source.

   - A) NO CHANGE

   - B) providing a clean, sustainable energy source.

   - C) providing a clean; sustainable energy source.

   - D) providing a clean, and sustainable energy sources.

39. Wind turbines harness the power of the wind to generate electricity without producing harmful emissions.

   - A) NO CHANGE

   - B) harnesses the power of the wind

   - C) harnesses the power of wind

   - D) harness the power of the wind,

40. Investing in renewable energy technologies is crucial for achieving a sustainable future.

   - A) NO CHANGE

- B) is crucial to achieving

- C) is crucial in achieving

- D) is crucial to achieve

Passage 11: The internet has revolutionized the way people communicate and access information. Social media platforms allow users to connect with friends and family, share updates, and discover new content. Online education has made learning more accessible to people around the world. However, the rise of the internet has also brought challenges, such as privacy concerns and the spread of misinformation.

41. The internet has revolutionized the way people communicate and access information.

- A) NO CHANGE

- B) access informations

- C) accesses information

- D) accessing information

42. Social media platforms allow users to connect with friends and family, share updates, and discover new content.

- A) NO CHANGE

- B) sharing updates

- C) share updating

- D) shared updates

43. Online education has made learning more accessible to people around the world.

- A) NO CHANGE

- B) learning more accessible for people

- C) learn more accessible to people

- D) learning more accessibly to people

44. However, the rise of the internet has also brought challenges, such as privacy concerns and the spread of misinformation.

- A) NO CHANGE

- B) such as, privacy concerns and the spread of misinformation.

- C) such as privacy concerns, and the spread of misinformation.

- D) such as privacy concerns and the spread, of misinformation.

Passage 12: In recent years, there has been a growing interest in sustainable fashion. Consumers are becoming more aware of the environmental impact of their clothing choices and are seeking out brands that prioritize sustainability. Sustainable fashion involves using eco-friendly materials, reducing waste, and ensuring fair labor practices. By supporting sustainable fashion, individuals can make a positive difference in the world.

45. In recent years, there has been a growing interest in sustainable fashion.

- A) NO CHANGE

- B) there has been growing interest

- C) there has been a grow interest

- D) there has been a growing interests

46. Consumers are becoming more aware of the environmental impact of their clothing choices and are seeking out brands that prioritize sustainability.

- A) NO CHANGE

- B) brands, that prioritize sustainability.

- C) brands that prioritize sustainability,

- D) brands that prioritize; sustainability.

47. Sustainable fashion involves using eco-friendly materials, reducing waste, and ensuring fair labor practices.

- A) NO CHANGE

- B) involving using eco-friendly materials

- C) involves using eco-friendly materials;

- D) involves using, eco-friendly materials

48. By supporting sustainable fashion, individuals can make a positive difference in the world.

- A) NO CHANGE

- B) difference to the world

- C) difference in the worlds

- D) difference for the world

Passage 13: The field of artificial intelligence (AI) is rapidly advancing, with new applications being developed across various industries. AI is being used to improve healthcare, enhance customer service, and optimize supply chain management. However, the rise of AI also raises ethical questions, such as the impact on employment and the potential for biased decision-making. It is important to address these concerns as AI continues to evolve.

49. The field of artificial intelligence (AI) is rapidly advancing, with new applications being developed across various industries.

- A) NO CHANGE

- B) are rapidly advancing,

- C) is rapid advancing,

- D) is rapidly advancing;

50. AI is being used to improve healthcare, enhance customer service, and optimize supply chain management.

- A) NO CHANGE

- B) enhance customer service;

- C) enhancing customer service,

- D) enhance customer services,

51. However, the rise of AI also raises ethical questions, such as the impact on employment and the potential for biased decision-making.

- A) NO CHANGE

- B) such as, the impact on employment and the potential for biased decision-making.

- C) such as the impact on employment, and the potential for biased decision-making.

- D) such as the impact on employment and the potential, for biased decision-making.

52. It is important to address these concerns as AI continues to evolve.

- A) NO CHANGE

- B) continue to evolve.

- C) continues to evolve,

- D) continue evolving.

Passage 14: The Great Barrier Reef is one of the most famous natural wonders of the world. Stretching over 2,300 kilometers, it is the largest coral reef system on the planet. The reef is home to a diverse array of marine life, including fish, sharks, and sea turtles. However, the Great Barrier Reef is under threat from climate change, pollution, and overfishing.

53. The Great Barrier Reef is one of the most famous natural wonders of the world.

- A) NO CHANGE

- B) of the worlds

- C) of the world,

- D) of worlds

54. Stretching over 2,300 kilometers, it is the largest coral reef system on the planet.

- A) NO CHANGE

- B) largest, coral reef system

- C) largest coral reef, system

- D) largest coral reef system, on the planet

55. The reef is home to a diverse array of marine life, including fish, sharks, and sea turtles.

- A) NO CHANGE

- B) fish, sharks and sea turtles

- C) fish sharks, and sea turtles

- D) fish; sharks and sea turtles

56. However, the Great Barrier Reef is under threat from climate change, pollution, and overfishing.

- A) NO CHANGE

- B) threats from climate change,

- C) under threats from climate change,

- D) under threat from climate change;

Passage 15: The history of aviation is marked by numerous milestones, from the Wright brothers' first flight to the development of commercial air travel. Advances in aviation technology have made air travel safer, faster, and more efficient. Today, airlines are exploring new ways to reduce their environmental impact, such as using biofuels and improving fuel efficiency. The future of aviation looks promising as technology continues to evolve.

57. The history of aviation is marked by numerous milestones, from the Wright brothers' first flight to the development of commercial air travel.

- A) NO CHANGE

- B) the development, of commercial air travel.

- C) the development of, commercial air travel.

- D) the development of commercial air travel;

58. Advances in aviation technology have made air travel safer, faster, and more efficient.

- A) NO CHANGE

- B) made air travel more safer,

- C) made air travel safer, faster and more efficient.

- D) made air travel safer, faster, and more efficiently.

59. Today, airlines are exploring new ways to reduce their environmental impact, such as using biofuels and improving fuel efficiency.

- A) NO CHANGE

- B) reduce their environmental impacts,

- C) reduce their environmental impact;

- D) reducing their environmental impact,

60. The future of aviation looks promising as technology continues to evolve.

   - A) NO CHANGE
   - B) continue to evolve.
   - C) continues to evolve,
   - D) continues evolving.

Passage 16: The benefits of regular physical exercise are well-documented. Exercise helps maintain a healthy weight, reduces the risk of chronic diseases, and improves mental health. Additionally, physical activity can boost energy levels and promote better sleep. Whether it's running, swimming, or yoga, finding an enjoyable form of exercise can make it easier to stay active.

61. The benefits of regular physical exercise are well-documented.

   - A) NO CHANGE
   - B) are well document.
   - C) are well documented;
   - D) are well documented.

62. Exercise helps maintain a healthy weight, reduces the risk of chronic diseases, and improves mental health.

   - A) NO CHANGE
   - B) reduces the risks of chronic diseases
   - C) reduce the risk of chronic diseases
   - D) reducing the risk of chronic diseases

63. Additionally, physical activity can boost energy levels and promote better sleep.

   - A) NO CHANGE
   - B) and promoting better sleep.
   - C) and promote, better sleep.
   - D) and promote better sleep;

140

64. Whether it's running, swimming, or yoga, finding an enjoyable form of exercise can make it easier to stay active.

- A) NO CHANGE

- B) it's running, swimming or yoga,

- C) its running, swimming, or yoga,

- D) it's running, swimming or yoga;

Passage 17: The importance of learning a second language cannot be overstated. Bilingualism offers numerous cognitive, social, and professional benefits. Learning a new language can enhance memory, improve multitasking skills, and increase cultural awareness. In today's globalized world, being able to communicate in multiple languages is a valuable asset.

65. The importance of learning a second language cannot be overstated.

- A) NO CHANGE

- B) can't be overstated.

- C) cannot be overstate.

- D) cannot be overstated;

66. Bilingualism offers numerous cognitive, social, and professional benefits.

- A) NO CHANGE

- B) numerous cognitive, social and professional benefits

- C) numerous, cognitive, social, and professional benefits

- D) numerous cognitive, social; and professional benefits

67. Learning a new language can enhance memory, improve multitasking skills, and increase cultural awareness.

- A) NO CHANGE

- B) improve multi-tasking skills,

- C) improve multitasking skills;

- D) improve multi-tasking skills;

68. In today's globalized world, being able to communicate in multiple languages is a valuable asset.

- A) NO CHANGE

- B) a valueable asset.

- C) a valuable asset,

- D) a valuable assets.

Passage 18: Water conservation is a critical issue in many parts of the world. With growing populations and increasing demand, the availability of fresh water is becoming a concern. Implementing water-saving measures, such as using low-flow fixtures and fixing leaks, can make a significant difference. By conserving water, we can help ensure that this vital resource is available for future generations.

69. Water conservation is a critical issue in many parts of the world.

- A) NO CHANGE

- B) in many parts of the worlds

- C) in many parts, of the world

- D) in many parts of worlds

70. With growing populations and increasing demand, the availability of fresh water is becoming a concern.

- A) NO CHANGE

- B) fresh waters is becoming

- C) fresh water is become

- D) fresh water is becoming,

71. Implementing water-saving measures, such as using low-flow fixtures and fixing leaks, can make a significant difference.

- A) NO CHANGE

- B) can make a significantly difference

- C) can make a significant differences

- D) can make, a significant difference

72. By conserving water, we can help ensure that this vital resource is available for future generations.

- A) NO CHANGE

- B) can help ensure that this vital resources

- C) can help to ensure that this vital resource

- D) can help ensuring that this vital resource

Passage 19: Urban gardening has gained popularity in recent years as more people seek to grow their own food and create green spaces in cities. Rooftop gardens, community plots, and vertical farming are just a few examples of how urban areas are transforming into productive and sustainable environments. These green spaces not only provide fresh produce but also improve air quality and reduce urban heat islands. By integrating nature into urban planning, cities can become healthier and more resilient.

73. Urban gardening has gained popularity in recent years as more people seek to grow their own food and create green spaces in cities.

   - A) have gained popularity in recent years as more people seeking to grow their own food

   - B) has been gaining popularity in recent years as more people seek to grow their own food

   - C) has gained popularity in recent years more people seek to grow their own food

   - D) has gained popularity in recent years, as more people seek to grow their own food

74. Rooftop gardens, community plots, and vertical farming are just a few examples of how urban areas are transforming into productive and sustainable environments.

   - A) are just a few examples of how urban areas transform into productive and sustainable environments

   - B) is just a few examples of how urban areas are transforming into productive and sustainable environments

   - C) are just a few examples of how urban areas have transformed into productive and sustainable environments

   - D) are just a few examples of how urban areas are transforming into productive and sustainable environments

75. These green spaces not only provide fresh produce but also improve air quality and reduce urban heat islands.

- A) provides fresh produce but also improves air quality and reduces urban heat islands

- B) provide fresh produce and improves air quality, reducing urban heat islands

- C) provide fresh produce but also improve air quality and reduce urban heat islands

- D) providing fresh produce and also improve air quality while reducing urban heat islands

76. By integrating nature into urban planning, cities can become healthier and more resilient.

- A) integrating nature into urban planning, healthier cities can become and more resilient

- B) integrate nature into urban planning, cities can become healthier and more resilient

- C) by integrating nature into urban planning, cities become healthier and more resilient

- D) integrating nature into urban planning, healthier and more resilient cities can become

Answers

1. **A)** NO CHANGE

2. **B)** were well-received

3. **C)** have made

4. **A)** NO CHANGE

5. **A)** NO CHANGE

6. **C)** continue

7. **A)** NO CHANGE

8. **A)** NO CHANGE

9. **D)** has led to

10. **C)** than they were

11. **A)** NO CHANGE

12. A) NO CHANGE

13. A) NO CHANGE

14. B) none of them have

15. C) views were more spectacular

16. A) NO CHANGE

17. A) NO CHANGE

18. A) NO CHANGE

19. C) experience

20. A) NO CHANGE

21. A) NO CHANGE

22. B) that have stood for centuries.

23. D) its own unique histories.

24. A) NO CHANGE

25. A) NO CHANGE

26. A) NO CHANGE

27. D) are able use

28. A) NO CHANGE

29. A) NO CHANGE

30. A) NO CHANGE

31. A) NO CHANGE

32. A) NO CHANGE

33. A) NO CHANGE

34. A) NO CHANGE

35. A) NO CHANGE

36. A) NO CHANGE

37. A) NO CHANGE

38. B) providing a clean, sustainable energy source.

39.A) NO CHANGE

40.B) is crucial to achieving

41.A) NO CHANGE

42.A) NO CHANGE

43.A) NO CHANGE

44.A) NO CHANGE

45.A) NO CHANGE

46.A) NO CHANGE

47.A) NO CHANGE

48.A) NO CHANGE

49.A) NO CHANGE

50.A) NO CHANGE

51.A) NO CHANGE

52.A) NO CHANGE

53.A) NO CHANGE

54.A) NO CHANGE

55.A) NO CHANGE

56.A) NO CHANGE

57.A) NO CHANGE

58.A) NO CHANGE

59.A) NO CHANGE

60.A) NO CHANGE

61.A) NO CHANGE

62.A) NO CHANGE

63.A) NO CHANGE

64.A) NO CHANGE

65.A) NO CHANGE

66. A) NO CHANGE

67. A) NO CHANGE

68. A) NO CHANGE

69. A) NO CHANGE

70. A) NO CHANGE

71. A) NO CHANGE

72. A) NO CHANGE

73. B) has been gaining popularity in recent years as more people seek to grow their own food

74. D) are just a few examples of how urban areas have transformed into productive and sustainable environments

75. C) provide fresh produce but also improve air quality and reduce urban heat islands

76. B) integrate nature into urban planning, cities can become healthier and more resilient

Section 2: Mathematics (60 Questions in 60 minutes)

1. If $5x + 3 = 23$, what is the value of x?

   - A) 4
   - B) 5
   - C) 6
   - D) 7
   - E) 8

2. What is the value of x in the equation $2(3x - 4) + 5 = 21$?

   - A) 2
   - B) 3
   - C) 4
   - D) 5
   - E) 6

3. What is the area of a triangle with a base of 10 units and a height of 5 units?

- A) 15
- B) 20
- C) 25
- D) 30
- E) 35

4. What is the solution to the equation $x^2 - 4x - 5 = 0$?

- A) -1, 5
- B) -5, 1
- C) 1, -5
- D) 5, -1
- E) 5, 1

5. What is the slope of the line that passes through the points (2, 3) and (4, 7)?

- A) 2
- B) 3
- C) 4
- D) 5
- E) 6

6. If $y = 2x + 3$, what is the value of y when x = 4?

- A) 5
- B) 7
- C) 9
- D) 11
- E) 13

7. If sqrt (49) = x, what is the value of x?

- A) 5

- B) 6
- C) 7
- D) 8
- E) 9

8. What is the perimeter of a rectangle with 8 units in length and 6 units in width?

   - A) 24
   - B) 26
   - C) 28
   - D) 30
   - E) 32

9. If 2^x = 16, what is the value of x?

   - A) 2
   - B) 3
   - C) 4
   - D) 5
   - E) 6

10. What is the solution to the equation 3x - 2 = 7?

   - A) 2
   - B) 3
   - C) 4
   - D) 5
   - E) 6

11. What is the circumference of a circle with a radius of 7 units? (Use π ≈ 3.14)

   - A) 22
   - B) 38.5
   - C) 44

- D) 48.1
- E) 50

12. If the area of a square is 64 square units, what is the length of a side?

- A) 6
- B) 7
- C) 8
- D) 9
- E) 10

13. What is the value of x in the equation 4x - 7 = 9?

- A) 2
- B) 3
- C) 4
- D) 5
- E) 6

14. What is the area of a circle with a radius of 5 units? (Use $\pi \approx 3.14$)

- A) 25π
- B) 78.5
- C) 31.4
- D) 50π
- E) 16π

15. If y = 3x - 4, what is the value of y when x = 5?

- A) 7
- B) 9
- C) 11
- D) 13
- E) 15

16. What is the volume of a cube with an edge of 3 units?

- A) 9

- B) 18

- C) 27

- D) 36

- E) 45

17. What is the solution to the equation 2x + 5 = 17?

- A) 4

- B) 5

- C) 6

- D) 7

- E) 8

18. If 3x - 4 = 11, what is the value of x?

- A) 4

- B) 5

- C) 6

- D) 7

- E) 8

19. If the perimeter of a square is 20 units, what is the length of a side?

- A) 3

- B) 4

- C) 5

- D) 6

- E) 7

20. What is the value of x in the equation $x^2 = 36$?

- A) 4
- B) 5
- C) 6
- D) 7
- E) 8

21. If $y = x^2 + 3x + 2$, what is the value of y when x = 2?

- A) 5
- B) 8
- C) 12
- D) 14
- E) 17

22. What is the slope of the line $y = 4x + 7$?

- A) 2
- B) 3
- C) 4
- D) 5
- E) 6

23. If $5x - 3 = 12$, what is the value of x?

- A) 2
- B) 3
- C) 4
- D) 5
- E) 6

24. What is the area of a rectangle with a length of 10 units and a width of 4 units?

- A) 20
- B) 30
- C) 40
- D) 50
- E) 60

25. If 2x + 3 = 13, what is the value of x?

- A) 4
- B) 5
- C) 6
- D) 7
- E) 8

26. What is the volume of a cylinder with a radius of 3 units and a height of 4 units? (Use $\pi \approx 3.14$)

- A) 36π
- B) 48π
- C) 72π
- D) 84π
- E) 113.04

27. If x^2 - 9 = 0, what is the value of x?

- A) -3, 3
- B) 0.3
- C) -3, 0
- D) 0, -3
- E) 3, -3

28. What is the value of x in the equation 4x - 3 = 9?

- A) 2
- B) 3
- C) 4
- D) 5
- E) 6

29. What is the value of x in the equation x^2 - 16 = 0?

- A) 2
- B) -4, 4
- C) 4
- D) -2, 2
- E) -4

30. If the perimeter of a triangle is 24 units and two of its sides measure 7 units each, how long is the third side?

- A) 8
- B) 9
- C) 10
- D) 11
- E) 12

31. What is the slope of the line that passes through the points (1, 2) and (3, 6)?

- A) 1
- B) 2
- C) 3
- D) 4
- E) 5

32. If y = 2x + 5, what is the value of y when x = 3?

- A) 7

- B) 9
- C) 11
- D) 13
- E) 15

33. What is the value of x in the equation 6x - 7 = 11?

- A) 2
- B) 3
- C) 4
- D) 5
- E) 6

34. What is the area of a triangle with a base of 8 units and a height of 4 units?

- A) 16
- B) 24
- C) 32
- D) 36
- E) 40

35. What is the value of x in the equation $x^2 + 6x + 9 = 0$?

- A) -3
- B) -2
- C) -1
- D) 0
- E) 1

36. If the area of a circle is 36π square units, what is the radius of the circle? (Use π ≈ 3.14)

- A) 4
- B) 5

- C) 6
- D) 7
- E) 8

37. What is the volume of a cube with an edge of 4 units?

- A) 16
- B) 32
- C) 48
- D) 64
- E) 80

38. If $7x + 2 = 23$, what is the value of x?

- A) 2
- B) 3
- C) 4
- D) 5
- E) 6

39. What is the value of x in the equation $8x - 5 = 27$?

- A) 2
- B) 3
- C) 4
- D) 5
- E) 6

40. What is the solution to the equation $x^2 - 1 = 0$?

- A) -1, 1
- B) 0, 1
- C) 1
- D) -1, 0

- E) 0, -1

41. What is the perimeter of a square with a side length of 9 units?

- A) 27

- B) 30

- C) 36

- D) 40

- E) 45

42. What is the slope of the line y = 3x + 2?

- A) 1

- B) 2

- C) 3

- D) 4

- E) 5

43. If 6x - 2 = 16, what is the value of x?

- A) 2

- B) 3

- C) 4

- D) 5

- E) 6

44. What is the value of x in the equation 5x + 7 = 22?

- A) 2

- B) 3

- C) 4

- D) 5

- E) 6

45. If the area of a triangle is 20 square units and its base measures 5 units, what is the height of the triangle?

- A) 5
- B) 6
- C) 7
- D) 8
- E) 9

46. What is the volume of a cylinder with a radius of 2 units and a height of 5 units? (Use $\pi \approx 3.14$)

- A) 19.6
- B) 23.7
- C) 34.3
- D) 40.5
- E) 62.8

47. If $x^2 - 4 = 0$, what is the value of x?

- A) -2, 2
- B) 0, 2
- C) -2, 0
- D) 0, -2
- E) 2, -2

48. What is the value of x in the equation $3x + 5 = 14$?

- A) 2
- B) 3
- C) 4
- D) 5
- E) 6

49. What is the area of a rectangle with a length of 12 units and a width of 5 units?

- A) 40
- B) 50
- C) 60
- D) 70
- E) 80

50. If 4x - 3 = 17, what is the value of x?

- A) 4
- B) 5
- C) 6
- D) 7
- E) 8

51. What is the value of x in the equation x^2 - 25 = 0?

- A) 5
- B) -5, 5
- C) -5
- D) 0.5
- E) 0, -5

52. If the perimeter of a triangle is 30 units and two of its sides measure 10 units each, how long is the third side?

- A) 8
- B) 9
- C) 10
- D) 11
- E) 12

53. What is the value of x in the equation 7x + 4 = 25?

- A) 2

- B) 3
- C) 4
- D) 5
- E) 6

54. What is the area of a circle with a radius of 6 units? (Use π ≈ 3.14)

- A) 36 π
- B) 113.04
- C) 72 π
- D) 78.5
- E) 16π

55. If $y = x^2 + 2x + 1$, what is the value of y when x = 3?

- A) 5
- B) 8
- C) 11
- D) 14
- E) 16

56. What is the slope of the line that passes through the points (2, 3) and (5, 11)?

- A) 2
- B) 3
- C) 4
- D) 5
- E) 6

57. If 3x + 4 = 13, what is the value of x?

- A) 2
- B) 3
- C) 4

- D) 5

- E) 6

58. What is the value of x in the equation 2x - 3 = 11?

  - A) 4

  - B) 5

  - C) 6

  - D) 7

  - E) 8

59. What is the volume of a cube with an edge of 5 units?

  - A) 25

  - B) 50

  - C) 75

  - D) 100

  - E) 125

60. What is the value of x in the equation x^2 + 2x - 8 = 0?

  - A) -4, 2

  - B) -2, 4

  - C) 2, -4

  - D) 4, -2

  - E) -2, -4

Answers

1. **A) 4**

Subtracting 3 from both sides gives 5x = 20. Dividing 20 by 5 gives x = 4.

2. **C) 4**

Expanding the equation gives 6x - 8 + 5 = 21. Simplifying it gives 6x - 3 = 21. Adding 3 to both sides gives 6x = 24. Dividing 24 by 6 gives x = 4.

3. C) 25

The area of a triangle is 1/2 * base * height = 1/2 * 10 * 5 = 25.

4. A) -1, 5

Factoring the equation gives (x - 5) (x + 1) = 0. The solutions are x = 5 and x = -1.

5. A) 2

The slope m = (y2 - y1) / (x2 - x1) = (7 - 3) / (4 - 2) = 4 / 2 = 2.

6. D) 11

Substituting x = 4 into y = 2x + 3 gives y = 2(4) + 3 = 8 + 3 = 11.

7. C) 7

The square root of 49 is 7.

8. C) 28

The perimeter of a rectangle is 2 * (length + width) = 2 * (8 + 6) = 2 * 14 = 28.

9. C) 4

2^4 = 16, therefore x = 4.

10. B) 3

Adding 2 to both sides gives 3x = 9. Dividing 9 by 3 gives x = 3.

11. C) 44

The circumference of a circle is 2πr = 2 * 3.14 * 7 ≈ 44.

12. C) 8

If the area is 64, the length of one side is sqrt (64) = 8.

13. C) 4

Adding 7 to both sides gives 4x = 16. Dividing 16 by 4 gives x = 4.

14. B) 78.5

The area of a circle is πr^2 = 3.14 * 5^2 = 3.14 * 25 = 78.5.

15. C) 11

Substituting x = 5 into y = 3x - 4 gives y = 3(5) - 4 = 15 - 4 = 11.

16. C) 27

The volume of a cube is side^3 = 3^3 = 27.

17. C) 6

Subtracting 5 from both sides gives $2x = 12$. Dividing 12 by 2 gives $x = 6$.

18. B) 5

Adding 4 to both sides gives $3x = 15$. Dividing 15 by 3 gives $x = 5$.

19. C) 5

The perimeter of a square is 4 * side. Dividing 20 by 4 gives side = 5.

20. C) 6

The square root of 36 is 6.

21. C) 12

Substituting $x = 2$ into $y = x^2 + 3x + 2$ gives $y = 2^2 + 3(2) + 2 = 4 + 6 + 2 = 12$.

22. C) 4

The slope of the line is the coefficient of x at $y = 4x + 7$.

23. B) 3

Adding 3 to both sides gives $5x = 15$. Dividing 15 by 5 gives $x = 3$.

24. C) 40

The area of a rectangle is length * width = 10 * 4 = 40.

25. B) 5

Subtracting 3 from both sides gives $2x = 10$. Dividing 10 by 2 gives $x = 5$.

26. E) 113.04

The volume of a cylinder is $\pi r^2 h$ = 3.14 * 3^2 * 4 = 3.14 * 9 * 4 = 113.04.

27. A) -3, 3

$x^2 - 9 = 0$ is factored as $(x + 3)(x - 3) = 0$, therefore $x = -3$ and $x = 3$.

28. B) 3

Adding 3 to both sides gives $4x = 12$. Dividing 12 by 4 gives $x = 3$.

29. B) -4, 4

$x^2 - 16 = 0$ is factored as $(x - 4)(x + 4) = 0$, therefore $x = 4$ and $x = -4$.

30. C) 10

The perimeter of a triangle is the sum of its sides. Subtracting 14 from 24 gives the third side = 10.

31. B) 2

The slope $m = (y_2 - y_1) / (x_2 - x_1) = (6 - 2) / (3 - 1) = 4 / 2 = 2$.

32. C) 11

Substituting $x = 3$ into $y = 2x + 5$ gives $y = 2(3) + 5 = 6 + 5 = 11$.

33. B) 3

Adding 7 to both sides gives $6x = 18$. Dividing 18 by 6 gives $x = 3$.

34. A) 16

The area of a triangle is $1/2 * base * height = 1/2 * 8 * 4 = 16$.

35. A) -3

The equation $x^2 + 6x + 9 = 0$ is factored as $(x + 3)^2 = 0$, therefore $x = -3$.

36. C) 6

The area of a circle is πr^2. If the area is 36π, then $r^2 = 36$, the square root of 36 is 6.

37. D) 64

The volume of a cube is $side^3 = 4^3 = 64$.

38. B) 3

Subtracting 2 from both sides gives $7x = 21$. Dividing 21 by 7 gives $x = 3$.

39. C) 4

Adding 5 to both sides gives $8x = 32$. Dividing 32 by 8 gives $x = 4$.

40. A) -1, 1

The equation $x^2 - 1 = 0$ is factored as $(x - 1)(x + 1) = 0$, therefore $x = 1$ and $x = -1$.

41. C) 36

The perimeter of a square is $4 * side$. If the side measures 9, then $4 * 9 = 36$ is the answer.

42. C) 3

The slope of the line is the coefficient of x at y = 3x + 2.

43. B) 3

Adding 2 to both sides gives 6x = 18. Dividing 18 by 6 gives x = 3.

44. B) 3

Subtracting 7 from both sides gives 5x = 15. Dividing 15 by 5 gives x = 3.

45. D) 8

The area of a triangle is 1/2 * base * height. If the area is 20 and the base is 5, then 1/2 * 5 * height = 20. Solving gives height = 8.

46. E) 62.8

The volume of a cylinder is πr^2h = 3.14 * 2^2 * 5 = 3.14 * 4 * 5 = 62.8.

47. A) -2, 2

The equation x^2 - 4 = 0 is factored as (x - 2) (x + 2) = 0, therefore x = 2 and x = -2.

48. B) 3

Subtracting 5 from both sides gives 3x = 9. Dividing 9 by 3 gives x = 3.

49. C) 60

The area of a rectangle is length * width = 12 * 5 = 60.

50. B) 5

Adding 3 to both sides gives 4x = 20. Dividing 20 by 4 gives x = 5.

51. B) -5, 5

The equation x^2 - 25 = 0 is factored as (x - 5) (x + 5) = 0, therefore x = 5 and x = -5.

52. C) 10

The perimeter of a triangle is the sum of its sides. If two sides measure 10 units each, then the third side is 30 - 20 = 10.

53. B) 3

Subtracting 4 from both sides gives 7x = 21. Dividing 21 by 7 gives x = 3.

54. B) 113.04

The area of a circle is πr^2 = 3.14 * 6^2 = 3.14 * 36 = 113.04.

55. E) 16

Substituting x = 3 into y = x^2 + 2x + 1 gives y = 3^2 + 2(3) + 1 = 9 + 6 + 1 = 16.

56. B) 3

The slope m = (y2 - y1) / (x2 - x1) = (11 - 3) / (5 - 2) = 8 / 3.

57. B) 3

Subtracting 4 from both sides gives 3x = 9. Dividing 9 by 3 gives x = 3.

58. D) 7

Adding 3 to both sides gives 2x = 14. Dividing 14 by 2 gives x = 7.

59. E) 125

The volume of a cube is side^3 = 5^3 = 125.

60. A) -4, 2

The equation x^2 + 2x - 8 = 0 is factored as (x + 4) (x - 2) = 0, therefore x = -4 and x = 2.

Section 3: Reading (40 Questions in 35 minutes)

Passage 1: On my grandparents' farm, there was always something new to learn. Since dawn, the rooster crowed announcing the start of the day. Corn crops stretched for hectares, and in the orchard, strawberries peeked out from the green leaves.

1. What is the grandfather's main occupation in the passage?

   - A) Livestock farmer

   - B) Farmer

   - C) Carpenter

   - D) Fisherman

2. What does the crowing of the rooster indicate in the passage?

   - A) The end of the day

   - B) The arrival of the night

   - C) The beginning of the day

   - D) Lunch time

3. What is grown on the farm besides corn?

- A) Apples

- B) Grapes

- C) Strawberries

- D) Carrots

Passage 2: The city was full of life. The lights of the buildings shone brightly, and the streets were packed with people. The yellow taxis moved quickly through the avenues, and the sound of their horns could be heard at every moment.

4. What does the passage describe?

- A) A quiet city

- B) An open field

- C) A city full of life

- D) A deserted beach

5. What color are the taxis mentioned in the passage?

- A) Red

- B) Blue

- C) Yellow

- D) Green

6. What is heard in the city according to the passage?

- A) The singing of birds

- B) The sound of the horns

- C) The murmur of the river

- D) The noise of the sea

Passage 3: The forest was a haven of peace. Tall, leafy trees offered shade, and birdsong filled the air. The path wound through the trees, guiding walkers toward a small crystalline lake.

7. What type of place does the passage describe?

- A) A desert

- B) A snowy mountain

- C) A forest

- D) A city

8. What did the trees in the forest offer?

   - A) Fruits

   - B) Flowers

   - C) Shadow

   - D) Wood

9. What did the path guide walkers toward?

   - A) A dark cave

   - B) A field of flowers

   - C) A small lake

   - D) A mountain

Passage 4: On the beach, the waves crashed gently against the shore. Children built sandcastles and adults lounged under colorful umbrellas. The sun shone brightly in the clear sky.

10. What did the children build on the beach?

    - A) Ships

    - B) Houses

    - C) Sand castles

    - D) Towers

11. What were adults doing on the beach?

    - A) They played volleyball

    - B) They swam

    - C) They rested under umbrellas

    - D) They surfed

12. What was heaven like according to the passage?

- A) Cloudy
- B) Clear
- C) Rainy
- D) Snowy

Passage 5: The museum was fascinating. The exhibits displayed ancient artifacts, and the walls were filled with famous paintings. The guide explained the story behind each piece with enthusiasm.

13. What did the exhibits in the museum show?

- A) Modern art
- B) Contemporary sculptures
- C) Ancient artifacts
- D) Photographs

14. What covered the walls of the museum?

- A) Maps
- B) Famous paintings
- C) Mirrors
- D) Posters

15. How did the guide explain the story behind each piece?

- A) with boredom
- B) with enthusiasm
- C) with sadness
- D) with indifference

Passage 6: The park was a meeting place. The benches were occupied by people reading or talking, and children were playing on the grass. The flowers were in full bloom, filling the air with their fragrance.

16. What were people doing on the park benches?

- A) They slept
- B) They read or talked

- C) They ate

- D) They worked

17. Where did the children play in the park?

- A) At the lake

- B) On the grass

- C) In the banks

- D) In the flowers

18. What filled the air in the park?

- A) The singing of birds

- B) The fragrance of flowers

- C) The sound of the source

- D) The traffic noise

Passage 7: The library was a sanctuary of silence. The shelves were filled with books of all genres, and the reading tables were occupied by students and avid readers. The soft light from the lamps created a cozy atmosphere.

19. How would you describe the atmosphere of the library?

- A) Noisy

- B) Silent

- C) Dark

- D) Messy

20. Who occupied the reading tables?

- A) Sellers

- B) Artists

- C) Students and avid readers

- D) Young children

21. What kind of light was in the library?

- A) Bright light

- B) Candlelight

- C) Soft light from lamps

- D) Natural light

Passage 8: The botanical garden was a spectacle of colors. The exotic flowers and rare plants attracted visitors from all over. Stone paths meandered through the flower beds, and every corner offered a stunning view.

22. What attracted visitors to the botanical garden?

- A) The animals

- B) The exotic flowers and rare plants

- C) The sources

- D) The wooden benches

23. What were the paths like in the botanical garden?

- A) Land

- B) Sand

- C) Stone

- D) Wood

24. What did each corner of the botanical garden offer?

- A) A place to rest

- B) An impressive view

- C) A souvenir shop

- D) A pond

Passage 9: The fair was a place of fun and excitement. Rides spun and climbed, and concession stands offered treats and refreshments. Colorful lights illuminated the place while music filled the air.

25. What did the food stalls offer at the fair?

- A) Fast food

- B) Sweets and soft drinks

- C) Gourmet dishes

- D) Alcoholic beverages

26. What did the mechanical attractions do at the fair?

- A) They turned and went up

- B) They went down and stopped

- C) They stayed still

- D) They moved slowly

27. What illuminated the fair?

- A) Colored lights

- B) Lanterns

- C) Candles

- D) Gas lamps

Passage 10: The mountain rose majestically on the horizon. The snow-capped peaks glistened in the sun, and the trails beckoned hikers to explore. The view from the top was spectacular.

28. What were the mountain peaks like?

- A) Rocky

- B) Snowy

- C) Green

- D) Desert

29. What did the mountain trails invite you to do?

- A) Swimming

- B) Camping

- C) Explore

- D) Scale

30. What was the view like from the top of the mountain?

- A) Challenging

- B) Dangerous

- C) Spectacular

- D) Boring

Passage 11: The zoo was a place full of life. Animals from different parts of the world lived in enclosures designed to imitate their natural environment. Visitors walked from place to place, marveling at the diversity of species.

31. What did the enclosures at the zoo imitate?

- A) The parks

- B) Homes

- C) The natural environment of the animals

- D) The gardens

32. How did the visitors feel at the zoo?

- A) Bored

- B) Amazed

- C) Tired

- D) Scared

33. What type of place does the passage describe?

- A) An amusement park

- B) A zoo

- C) An aquarium

- D) A nature reserve

Passage 12: The theater was full of excitement. The lights went out and the curtain rose, revealing the actors on stage. The audience watched silently, captivated by the story unfolding before their eyes.

34. What happened when the lights went out in the theater?

- A) People came out

- B) The curtain rose

- C) The actors left
- D) The music started

35. How was the audience in the theater?

- A) Noisy
- B) Captivated
- C) Boring
- D) Distracted

36. What was revealed when the curtain rose?

- A) The musicians
- B) The decoration
- C) The actors
- D) The public

Passage 13: The lake reflected the blue sky and the surrounding mountains. Birds flew over the water, and fish swam near the shore. People enjoyed boat rides and picnics on the shore.

37. What did the lake reflect?

- A) The trees
- B) The birds
- C) The blue sky and the mountains
- D) The houses

38. What were people doing at the lake?

- A) They swam
- B) They rode boats and made picnics
- C) They fished
- D) They camped

39. Where did the fish swim according to the passage?

- A) In the center of the lake

- B) Near the shore
- C) Underwater
- D) On the surface

Passage 14: The town square was the heart of the community. The shops and cafes were bustling with people, and the open-air market offered fresh produce. The children ran and played while the adults talked.

40. What did the open-air market in the town square offer?

- A) Clothing
- B) Electronics
- C) Fresh products
- D) Toys

Answers

1: B) Farmer

Grandfather works on a farm growing corn and strawberries, indicating that his main occupation is agriculture.

2: C) The beginning of the day

The passage mentions that the crowing of the rooster announces the beginning of the day.

3: C) Strawberries

The passage mentions that, in addition to corn, strawberries are grown in the garden.

4: C) A city full of life

The passage describes a city with bright lights, crowded streets, and moving taxis, indicating a city full of life.

5: C) Yellow

The passage mentions that taxis are yellow.

6: B) The sound of the horns

The passage points out that the sound of horns is heard in the city.

7: C) A forest

The passage describes tall trees, birdsong, and a path leading to a lake, indicating that the location is a forest.

8: C) Shadow

Tall, leafy trees offered shade.

9: C) A small lake

The passage mentions that the path guides walkers towards a small lake.

10: C) Sand castles

The passage says that children build sandcastles on the beach.

11: C) They rested under umbrellas

The passage mentions that adults rested under colorful umbrellas.

12: B) Clear

The passage mentions that the sun was shining in the clear sky.

13: C) Ancient artifacts

The passage says that the exhibits displayed ancient artifacts.

14: B) Famous paintings

The passage mentions that the walls were full of famous paintings.

15: B) With enthusiasm

The passage mentions that the guide explained the story behind each piece with enthusiasm.

16: B) They read or talked

The passage mentions that the benches were occupied by people reading or talking.

17: B) On the grass

The passage mentions that the children played on the grass.

18: B) The fragrance of flowers

The passage mentions that the flowers were in full bloom, filling the air with their fragrance.

19: B) Silent

The passage describes the library as a sanctuary of silence.

20: C) Students and avid readers

The passage mentions that the reading tables were occupied by Students and avid readers.

21: C) Soft light from lamps

The passage mentions that the soft light of the lamps created a welcoming atmosphere.

22: B) Exotic flowers and rare plants

The passage mentions that exotic flowers and rare plants attracted visitors from all over.

23: C) Of stone

The passage mentions that stone paths wound between the flower beds.

24: B) An impressive view

The passage mentions that every corner offered a breathtaking view.

25: B) Sweets and soft drinks

The passage mentions that food stalls offered sweets and refreshments.

26: A) They turned and went up

The passage mentions that the rides turned and went up.

27: A) Colored lights

The passage mentions that colored lights illuminated the fair.

28: B) Snowy

The passage mentions that the snow-capped peaks shone in the sun.

29: C) Explore

The passage mentions that trails invited hikers to explore.

30: C) Spectacular

The passage mentions that the view from the top was spectacular.

31: C) The natural environment of the animals

The passage mentions that the enclosures at the zoo were designed to mimic the animals' natural environment.

32: B) Amazed

The passage mentions that the visitors were amazed by the diversity of species.

33: B) A zoo

The passage describes a zoo.

34: B) The curtain rose

The passage mentions that the lights went out and the curtain rose.

35: B) Captivated

The passage mentions that the audience watched silently, captivated by the story.

36: C) The actors

The passage mentions that when the curtain rose, the actors on the stage were revealed.

37: C) The blue sky and the mountains

The passage mentions that the lake reflected the blue sky and the surrounding mountains.

38: B) Boat rides and picnics

The passage mentions that people enjoyed boat rides and picnics on the shore.

39: B) Near the shore

The passage mentions that the fish swam close to the shore.

40: C) Fresh products

The passage mentions that the open-air market offered fresh produce.

Section 4: Science (40 Questions in 35 minutes)

Passage 1: A group of scientists studied the effect of different concentrations of fertilizers on the growth of a plant. The scientists prepared four groups of plants: Group A received pure water, Group B received a solution with 10% fertilizer, Group C received a solution with 20% fertilizer, and Group D received a solution with 30% fertilizer. After 8 weeks, the height of the plants was measured.

Results Table:

Cluster	Average Height (inches)
Group A	4.72
Group B	7.09
Group C	9.45
Group D	11.81

1. Which group of plants grew the tallest?

   - A) Group A

   - B) Group B

   - C) Group C

   - D) Group D

2. What is the difference in average height between Group B and Group C?

   - A) 1.57 inches

   - B) 2.36 inches

   - C) 3.15 inches

   - D) 3.94 inches

3. What variable was manipulated in the experiment?

   - A) The type of plant

   - B) The amount of water

   - C) The concentration of fertilizer

   - D) The temperature

Passage 2: The effect of temperature on the solubility of a solid in water was investigated. Experiments were carried out at different temperatures and the amount of solid that dissolved in 100 ml of water was measured.

Results Table:

Temperature (°F)	Solubility (g/100 ml)
32	30

Temperature (°F)	Solubility (g/100 ml)
68	60
104	90
140	120
176	150
212	180

4. What temperature showed the greatest solubility of the solid?

- A) 32°F

- B) 68°F

- C) 140°F

- D) 212°F

5. How does temperature affect the solubility of the solid?

- A) Decreases it

- B) Increases it

- C) Keeps it constant

- D) Has no effect

6. If the temperature increases from 68°F to 104°F, how much does the solubility increase?

- A) 20 g/100 ml

- B) 30 g/100 ml

- C) 40 g/100 ml

- D) 60 g/100 ml

Passage 3: An experiment was conducted to observe the effect of light on oxygen production by aquatic plants. Three groups of aquatic plants were exposed to different light intensities for 6 hours. Group X was exposed to low light, Group Y to medium light, and Group Z to high light. The amount of oxygen produced was measured.

Results Table:

Cluster	Light Intensity	Produced Oxygen (mg/h)
Group X	Low	10
Group Y	Medium	20
Group Z	High	30

7. Which group produced more oxygen?

   - A) Group X

   - B) Group Y

   - C) Group Z

   - D) They all produced the same

8. How does light intensity affect oxygen production?

   - A) Decreases it

   - B) Increases it

   - C) Keeps it constant

   - D) Has no effect

9. What variable was measured in the experiment?

   - A) The intensity of the light

   - B) The type of aquatic plant

   - C) The amount of oxygen produced

   - D) The exposure time

Passage 4: The relationship between soil pH and nutrient absorption by plants was studied. Four soil samples were prepared with different pH levels: 4, 5, 6, and 7. Seeds were planted in each sample and the amount of nutrients absorbed was measured after 4 weeks.

Results Table:

Soil pH	Nutrients Absorbed (mg)
4	5
5	10
6	15
7	20

10. What soil pH resulted in the greatest nutrient absorption?

- A) 4
- B) 5
- C) 6
- D) 7

11. What variable was manipulated in the experiment?

- A) The type of plant
- B) The pH of the soil
- C) The amount of water
- D) The temperature

12. How does soil pH affect nutrient absorption?

- A) Decreases it
- B) Increases it
- C) Keeps it constant
- D) Has no effect

Passage 5: One study looked at the relationship between the amount of sleep and academic performance. 100 students were surveyed and their grade point average was recorded along with the number of hours of sleep per night.

Results Table:

Sleep Hours	Qualifies as Average
4	70

Sleep Hours	Qualifies as Average
5	75
6	80
7	85
8	90
9	95

13. How many hours of sleep are associated with the highest GPA?

- A) 4
- B) 6
- C) 8
- D) 9

14. How does the amount of sleep affect GPA?

- A) Decreases it
- B) Increases it
- C) Keeps it constant
- D) Has no effect

15. What variable was measured?

- A) The number of students
- B) The number of hours of sleep
- C) The academic performance (grade point average)
- D) The age of the students

Passage 6: An experiment was conducted to investigate the effect of different types of music on concentration while studying. Three groups of students listened to classical music, rock music, and no music while solving math problems. The time it took to solve the problems was recorded.

Results Table:

Cluster	Kind of Music	Average Time (minutes)
Group A	Classic	20
Group B	Rock	25
Group C	Without music	15

16. Which group took the least time to solve the problems?

- A) Group A

- B) Group B

- C) Group C

- D) They all took the same time

17. How does rock music affect concentration compared to not listening to music?

- A) Increases the concentration

- B) Decreases the concentration

- C) Keeps it constant

- D) Has no effect

18. What variable was measured in the experiment?

- A) The type of music

- B) The number of students

- C) The average time to solve problems

- D) The type of mathematical problems

Passage 7: A study was conducted to determine the effect of sun exposure time on vitamin D production in the human body. Four groups of participants were selected and each group was exposed to the sun for different periods: 15, 30, 45, and 60 minutes. The amount of vitamin D produced after exposure was measured.

Results Table:

Exposure Time (minutes)	Vitamin D Production (ng/ml)
15	10

Exposure Time (minutes)	Vitamin D Production (ng/ml)
30	20
45	30
60	40

19. Which group produced the most vitamin D?

- A) 15 minutes

- B) 30 minutes

- C) 45 minutes

- D) 60 minutes

20. How does sun exposure time affect vitamin D production?

- A) Decreases it

- B) Increases it

- C) Keeps it constant

- D) Has no effect

21. What variable was manipulated in the experiment?

- A) The amount of vitamin D

- B) The type of participants

- C) The time of sun exposure

- D) The age of the participants

Passage 8: The relationship between wind speed and power generation in a wind turbine was investigated. The levels of energy generated at different wind speeds were measured.

Results Table:

Wind Speed (mph)	Generated Energy (kWh)
6.21	50
12.43	100

Wind Speed (mph)	Generated Energy (kWh)
18.64	150
24.85	200
31.07	250

22. What wind speed resulted in the most power generation?

- A) 6.21 mph
- B) 12.43 mph
- C) 18.64 mph
- D) 31.07 mph

23. How does wind speed affect power generation?

- A) Decreases it
- B) Increases it
- C) Keeps it constant
- D) Has no effect

24. What variable was measured in the experiment?

- A) The speed of the wind
- B) The type of turbine
- C) The energy generated
- D) The location of the turbine

Passage 9: An experiment was performed to analyze the effect of particle size on the rate of dissolution in water. Large, medium, and small particles were used and the time they took to dissolve was measured.

Results Table:

Particle Size	Dissolution Time (minutes)
Big	30
Medium	20

Particle Size	Dissolution Time (minutes)
Small	10

25. What size particle dissolved the fastest?

- A) Large

- B) Medium

- C) Small

- D) They all dissolved at the same time

26. How does particle size affect dissolution rate?

- A) The larger the size, the higher the dissolution rate

- B) The smaller the size, the higher the dissolution rate

- C) The size does not affect the dissolution rate

- D) There is no clear pattern

27. What variable was measured in the experiment?

- A) The type of particles

- B) The dissolution time

- C) The amount of water

- D) The temperature of the water

Passage 10: An experiment was conducted to analyze the effect of different types of soil on the growth of the roots of a plant. Three types of soil were tested: sandy, clay, and loam. Root length was measured after 6 weeks.

Results Table:

Soil Type	Root Length (Inches)
Sandy	3.94
Clay	1.97
Loam	5.91

28. What type of soil allowed the most root growth?

- A) Sandy

- B) Clay

- C) Loam

- D) They were all the same

29. How does soil type affect root growth?

  - A) Sandy soil allows the greatest growth

  - B) Clay soil allows the greatest growth

  - C) Loam soil allows the greatest growth

  - D) Soil type does not affect growth

30. What variable was manipulated in the experiment?

  - A) The type of plant

  - B) The amount of water

  - C) The type of soil

  - D) The temperature

Passage 11: The relationship between study time and test results was investigated. 50 students were surveyed and study time and test scores were recorded.

Results Table:

Study Time (hours)	Exam Scores
1	50
2	60
3	70
4	80
5	90

31. How much study time was associated with the highest test score?

  - A) 1 hour

  - B) 3 hours

- C) 4 hours

- D) 5 hours

32. How does study time affect test scores?

- A) Decreases it

- B) Increases it

- C) Keeps it constant

- D) Has no effect

33. What variable was measured in the study?

- A) The number of students

- B) The study time

- C) The score on the test

- D) The difficulty of the test

Passage 12: A study investigated the effect of different humidity levels on the rate of water evaporation. Water samples were prepared and evaporation time was measured at humidity levels of 20%, 40%, 60%, and 80%.

Results Table:

Humidity Level (%)	Evaporation Time (minutes)
20	30
40	40
60	50
80	60

34. Which humidity level showed the longest evaporation time?

- A) 20%

- B) 40%

- C) 60%

- D) 80%

35. How does humidity level affect the evaporation rate?

- A) The higher the humidity, the higher the evaporation rate

- B) The higher the humidity, the lower the evaporation rate

- C) Humidity does not affect the evaporation rate

- D) There is no clear pattern

36. What variable was manipulated in the experiment?

- A) The amount of water

- B) The humidity level

- C) The temperature

- D) The evaporation time

Passage 13: A study was conducted to observe the effect of type of light on the growth of bacteria. Three groups of bacteria were exposed to white light, blue light, and no light. Bacterial growth was measured after 24 hours.

Results Table:

Light Type	Bacterial Growth (Inches)
White	0.59
Blue	0.39
Without light	0.20

37. What type of light resulted in the most bacterial growth?

- A) White light

- B) Blue light

- C) No light

- D) They were all the same

38. How does blue light affect bacterial growth compared to no light?

- A) Increases growth

- B) Decreases growth

- C) Keeps it constant

- D) Has no effect

39. What variable was measured in the experiment?

- A) The type of bacteria

- B) The type of light

- C) The bacterial growth

- D) The exposure time

Passage 14: The relationship between the amount of caffeine and the level of alertness in the test subjects was investigated. Four groups of subjects received 0 mg, 50 mg, 100 mg, and 150 mg of caffeine. Their alertness level was measured after 1 hour.

Results Table:

Amount of Caffeine (mg)	Alert Level
0	Low
50	Moderate
100	High
150	Very high

40. Which group showed the highest level of alertness?

- A) 0 mg

- B) 50 mg

- C) 100 mg

- D) 150 mg

Answers

1. D) Group D

Group D, which received the solution with 30% fertilizer, had the highest average height of 11.81 inches.

2. B) 2.36 inches

The difference in average height between Group B (7.09 inches) and Group C (9.45 inches) is 2.36 inches.

3. C) Fertilizer concentration

The variable manipulated in the experiment was the fertilizer concentration.

4. D) 212°F

At 212°F, the solubility of the solid is 180 g/100 ml, the highest solubility recorded.

5. B) It increases

As the temperature increases, the solubility of the solid also increases.

6. B) 30 g/100 ml

The solubility increases from 60 g/100 ml to 90 g/100 ml when the temperature goes from 68°F to 104°F.

7. C) Group Z

Group Z, exposed to high light, produced the greatest amount of oxygen (30 mg/h).

8. B) It increases

As light intensity increases, oxygen production also increases.

9. C) The amount of oxygen produced

The variable measured in the experiment was the amount of oxygen produced.

10. D) 7

Soil pH 7 resulted in the highest nutrient absorption (20 mg).

11. B) The pH of the soil

The variable manipulated in the experiment was soil pH.

12. B) It increases

As soil pH increases, nutrient uptake also increases.

13. D) 9

9 hours of sleep was associated with the highest GPA (95).

14. B) Increases it

As the amount of sleep increases, so does the GPA.

15. C) Academic performance (grade point average)

The variable measured in the study was academic performance (grade point average).

16. C) Group C

Group C, who did not listen to music, took less time to solve the problems (15 minutes).

17. B) Concentration decreases

Listening to rock music increased the average time to solve problems, indicating a decrease in concentration.

18. C) The average time to solve problems

The variable measured in the experiment was the average time to solve problems.

19. D) 60 minutes

The group exposed to the sun for 60 minutes produced the highest amount of vitamin D (40 ng/ml).

20. B) It increases

As time spent in the sun increases, vitamin D production also increases.

21. C) Sun exposure time

The variable manipulated in the experiment was the time of exposure to the sun.

22. D) 31.07 mph

The wind speed of 31.07 mph resulted in the highest power generation (250 kWh).

23. B) It increases

As wind speed increases, power generation also increases.

24. C) The energy generated

The variable measured in the experiment was the energy generated.

25. C) Small

Small particles dissolved faster (10 minutes).

26. B) The smaller the size, the higher the dissolution rate

The smaller particles dissolved faster than the larger particles.

27. B) Dissolution time

The variable measured in the experiment was the dissolution time.

28. C) Frank

The loam soil allowed the greatest root growth (5.91 inches).

29. C) Loam soil allows the greatest growth

The loam soil type allowed the greatest root growth.

30. C) The type of soil

The variable manipulated in the experiment was the type of soil.

31. D) 5 hours

5 hours of study was associated with the highest test score (90).

32. B) It increases it

As study time increases, test scores also increase.

33. C) The score on the test

The variable measured in the study was the score on the test.

34. D) 80%

The 80% humidity level showed the longest evaporation time (60 minutes).

35. B) The higher the humidity, the lower the evaporation rate

As the humidity level increases, the evaporation rate decreases, resulting in a longer evaporation time.

36. B) The humidity level

The variable manipulated in the experiment was the humidity level.

37. A) White light

White light resulted in the greatest bacterial growth (0.59 inches).

38. B) Growth decreases

Blue light resulted in less bacterial growth compared to no light.

39. C) Bacterial growth

The variable measured in the experiment was bacterial growth.

40. D) 150 mg

The group that received 150 mg of caffeine showed the highest level of alertness (very high).

ACT 2 Simulation Test

Section 1: English (75 Questions in 45 minutes)

Passage 1: Technology has transformed the way people communicate. The advent of smartphones has made it possible for individuals to stay connected wherever they are. Social media platforms allow instant for sharing of photos, videos, and messages, creating a global network of friends and acquaintances. However, this constant connectivity can also lead to distractions and a lack of privacy.

1. Technology has transformed the way people communicate.

    - A) transforming

    - B) has transformed

    - C) has transforming

    - D) is transformed

2. The advent of smartphones has made it possible for individuals to stay connected no matter where they are.

    - A) it has possible for individuals to stay

    - B) made possible for individuals to stay

    - C) made it possible for individuals stay

    - D) has made possible for individuals to stay

3. Social media platforms allow for instant sharing of photos, videos, and messages, creating a global network of friends and acquaintances.

    - A) instant share

    - B) instantly sharing

    - C) instantly share

    - D) allow instant sharing

4. However, this constant connectivity can also lead to distractions and a lack of privacy.

    - A) distraction and a lack of privacy

195

- B) distractions and lacks of privacy

- C) distraction and lacks of privacy

- D) distractions and a lack of privacies

Passage 2: The art of painting has evolved significantly over the centuries. Early artists used natural pigments to create their works, while modern artists have access to a wide range of synthetic materials. This evolution has allowed for greater creativity and experimentation. Many contemporary painters explore abstract concepts and techniques, pushing the boundaries of traditional art.

5. The art of painting has evolved significantly over the centuries.

- A) significant

- B) significantly evolving

- C) evolve significantly

- D) has significantly evolved

6. Early artists used natural pigments to create their works, while modern artists have access to a wide range of synthetic materials.

- A) accessing

- B) has accessed

- C) have access

- D) accessed

7. This evolution has allowed for greater creativity and experimentation.

- A) have allowed for

- B) allow for

- C) has allowing for

- D) allows for

8. Many contemporary painters explore abstract concepts and techniques, pushing the boundaries of traditional art.

- A) explored

- B) explores

- C) have explored

- D) has explored

Passage 3: The history of the bicycle is a fascinating one, filled with innovation and creativity. The first bicycles were simple wooden structures, but over time they have become more complex and efficient. Modern bicycles are made with lightweight materials and advanced engineering, making them faster and more comfortable to ride. Bicycling has become a popular form of transportation and recreation around the world.

9. The history of the bicycle is a fascinating one, filled with innovation and creativity.

    - A) fascinating ones, filled

    - B) fascinating, one filled

    - C) fascinating one, filled

    - D) fascination one filled

10. The first bicycles were simple wooden structures, but over time they have become more complex and efficient.

    - A) over time they became more complex

    - B) over time they has become more complex

    - C) over time, they have become more complex

    - D) over time, they becoming more complex

11. Modern bicycles are made with lightweight materials and advanced engineering, making them faster and more comfortable to ride.

    - A) and advancedly engineering

    - B) and advanced engineerings

    - C) and advancedly engineered

    - D) and advanced engineering

12. Bicycling has become a popular form of transportation and recreation around the world.

    - A) form of transportation and recreational around

    - B) form of transportation and recreations around

- C) form of transportation and recreational

- D) forms of transportation and recreation around

Passage 4: Renewable energy sources are crucial for the future of our planet. Solar power harnesses the energy of the sun to generate electricity, reducing reliance on fossil fuels. Wind power, too, offers a clean and sustainable alternative to traditional energy sources. As technology advances, the efficiency and accessibility of renewable energy will continue to improve.

13. Renewable energy sources are crucial for the future of our planet.

- A) crucially for the future

- B) crucial for the future

- C) crucial to the future

- D) crucially to the future

14. Solar power harnesses the energy of the sun to generate electricity, reducing reliance on fossil fuels.

- A) reliance of fossil fuels

- B) reliance in fossil fuels

- C) reliance on fossil fuel

- D) reliance on fossil fuels

15. Wind power, too, offers a clean and sustainable alternative to traditional energy sources.

- A) a cleanly and sustainable

- B) a clean and sustainably

- C) a clean and sustaining

- D) a clean and sustainable

16. As technology advances, the efficiency and accessibility of renewable energy will continue to improve.

- A) continues to improve

- B) will continue improving

- C) continue to improve

- D) continues improving

Passage 5: The benefits of regular exercise are well-documented. Exercise helps to maintain a healthy weight, strengthens the cardiovascular system, and improves mental health. Additionally, physical activity can boost mood and energy levels. Whether it's running, swimming, or lifting weights, finding a form of exercise that you enjoy can make it easier to stay active.

17. The benefits of regular exercise are well-documented.

- A) is well-documented
- B) are well-document
- C) is well-document
- D) are well-documented

18. Exercise helps to maintain a healthy weight, strengthens the cardiovascular system, and improves mental health.

- A) strengthen
- B) strengthens
- C) has strengthened
- D) have strengthened

19. Additionally, physical activity can boost mood and energy levels.

- A) can boosting
- B) can boosts
- C) can boost
- D) can boosted

20. Whether it's running, swimming, or lifting weights, finding a form of exercise that you enjoy can make it easier to stay active.

- A) its running, swimming, or lifting weights,
- B) it is running, swimming, or lifting weights,
- C) it running, swimming, or lifting weights,
- D) it's running, swimming, or lifting weights,

Passage 6: The role of technology in education is expanding rapidly. Digital tools have become an integral part of the learning process, providing students with access to a wealth of information. Online courses and educational apps offer flexible learning options, allowing individuals to study at their own pace. However, the digital divide remains a significant challenge, with some students lacking access to necessary technology.

21. The role of technology in education is expanding rapidly.

- A) expand rapidly

- B) expanding rapid

- C) expanded rapidly

- D) expanding rapidly

22. Digital tools have become an integral part of the learning process, providing students with access to a wealth of information.

- A) providing students access to a wealth of information

- B) providing students with access of a wealth of information

- C) providing students to access to a wealth of information

- D) providing students with access to a wealth of information

23. Online courses and educational apps offer flexible learning options, allowing individuals to study at their own pace.

- A) offer flexible learn options

- B) offers flexible learning options

- C) offer flexibly learning options

- D) offer flexible learning options

24. However, the digital divide remains a significant challenge, with some students lacking access to necessary technology.

- A) remains significant challenge

- B) remain a significant challenge

- C) remaining a significant challenge

- D) remains a significant challenge

Passage 7: The concept of time management is essential for achieving success in both personal and professional life. Efficient time management allows individuals to prioritize tasks and maximize productivity. Tools such as calendars and to-do lists can help in organizing one's schedule. By managing time effectively, stress can be reduced and goals can be accomplished more easily.

25. The concept of time management is essential for achieving success in both personal and professional life.

    - A) is essential to achieving
    - B) are essential for achieving
    - C) is essential for achieved
    - D) is essential for achieving

26. Efficient time management allows individuals to prioritize tasks and maximize productivity.

    - A) allow
    - B) is allowed
    - C) allows
    - D) are allowing

27. Tools such as calendars and to-do lists can help in organizing one's schedule.

    - A) help in organizing ones schedule
    - B) help to organize one's schedule
    - C) help organizing one's schedule
    - D) can help in organizing one's schedule

28. By managing time effectively, stress can be reduced and goals can be accomplished more easily.

    - A) stress can reduce and goals can accomplish
    - B) stress can be reduced and goals can accomplish
    - C) stress can reduce and goals can be accomplished
    - D) stress can be reduced and goals can be accomplished

Passage 8: Traveling to new places can provide a wealth of experiences and memories. Exploring different cultures, trying new foods, and meeting new people can broaden one's perspective and enhance personal growth. While traveling can sometimes be challenging, the benefits far outweigh the difficulties. Each journey can be an opportunity to learn and grow.

29. Traveling to new places can provide a wealth of experiences and memories.

- A) wealth of experience and memories
- B) wealth of experiences and memory
- C) wealths of experiences and memories
- D) a wealth of experiences and memories

30. Exploring different cultures, trying new foods, and meeting new people can broaden one's perspective and enhance personal growth.

- A) broadens
- B) broadening
- C) broadening and enhance
- D) broadens and enhances

31. While traveling can sometimes be challenging, the benefits far outweigh the difficulties.

- A) can sometimes challenging
- B) can sometimes been challenging
- C) can sometimes be challenged
- D) can sometimes be challenging

32. Each journey can be an opportunity to learn and grow.

- A) an opportunity to learned and grow
- B) an opportunity to learn and grew
- C) an opportunity to learning and grow
- D) an opportunity to learn and grow

Passage 9: Music has the power to evoke a wide range of emotions. Listening to a favorite song can bring back memories and create a sense of nostalgia. Music can also be a source of motivation and inspiration. Whether it's classical, rock, or pop, music plays an important role in many people's lives.

33. Music has the power to evoke a wide range of emotions.

   - A) has the power to evoking

   - B) have the power to evoke

   - C) having the power to evoke

   - D) evokes

34. Listening to a favorite song can bring back memories and create a sense of nostalgia.

   - A) bring back memory

   - B) brings back memories

   - C) bring backs memories

   - D) bringing back memories

35. Music can also be a source of motivation and inspiration.

   - A) a source of motivations and inspiration

   - B) a source of motivation and inspirations

   - C) a source of motivations and inspirations

   - D) a source of motivation and inspiration

36. Whether it's classical, rock, or pop, music plays an important role in many people's lives.

   - A) lives of many people

   - B) people's many lives

   - C) many people's live

   - D) many people's lives

Passage 10: The field of astronomy has fascinated humans for centuries. Ancient civilizations used the stars to navigate and to mark the passage of time. Today, astronomers use advanced technology to explore the universe and to understand its many mysteries. Telescopes, satellites, and space probes have expanded our knowledge of the cosmos.

37. The field of astronomy has fascinated humans for centuries.

- A) for century

- B) for centuries, fascinating

- C) for centuries, fascinates

- D) fascinates humans for centuries

38. Ancient civilizations used the stars to navigate and to mark the passage of time.

- A) civilizations used stars

- B) civilizations used the star

- C) civilizations used to navigate

- D) civilizations uses the stars

39. Today, astronomers use advanced technology to explore the universe and to understand its many mysteries.

- A) Today astronomers use

- B) Today, astronomers using

- C) Today, astronomers uses

- D) Today, astronomers use

40. Telescopes, satellites, and space probes have expanded our knowledge of the cosmos.

- A) have expanded our knowledge of cosmos

- B) has expanded our knowledge of the cosmos

- C) have expand our knowledge of the cosmos

- D) had expanded our knowledge of the cosmos

Passage 11: The benefits of a balanced diet are numerous. Eating a variety of fruits and vegetables provides essential vitamins and minerals. Whole grains, lean proteins, and healthy fats contribute to overall health and well-being. Maintaining a balanced diet can help prevent chronic diseases and support a healthy immune system.

41. The benefits of a balanced diet are numerous.

- A) is numerous
- B) are numerous.
- C) is numerous.
- D) is many

42. Eating a variety of fruits and vegetables provides essential vitamins and minerals.

  - A) provide essential vitamins and minerals
  - B) providing essential vitamins and minerals
  - C) provides essential vitamins and mineral
  - D) provides the essential vitamins and minerals

43. Whole grains, lean proteins, and healthy fats contribute to overall health and well-being.

  - A) contribute to overall health and well-beings
  - B) contribute to overall health and well-being
  - C) contributing to overall health and well-being
  - D) contributed to overall health and well-being

44. Maintaining a balanced diet can help prevent chronic diseases and support a healthy immune system.

  - A) supports
  - B) supporting
  - C) supports and preventing
  - D) prevent

Passage 12: The history of cinema is rich with innovation and creativity. Early filmmakers experimented with techniques such as stop-motion animation and special effects. Today, digital technology has revolutionized the industry, allowing for stunning visual effects and immersive storytelling. The future of cinema looks bright as filmmakers continue to push the boundaries of what is possible.

45. The history of cinema is rich with innovation and creativity.

  - A) was rich with innovation and creativity

- B) is rich with innovating and creativity

- C) is rich with innovation and creative

- D) has rich innovation and creativity

46. Early filmmakers experimented with techniques such as stop-motion animation and special effects.

   - A) experiment with techniques

   - B) experimented techniques

   - C) experiment with technique

   - D) experimented with techniques

47. Today, digital technology has revolutionized the industry, allowing for stunning visual effects and immersive storytelling.

   - A) has revolutionized industry

   - B) has revolutionized the industries

   - C) has revolutionize the industry

   - D) has revolutionized the industry

48. The future of cinema looks bright as filmmakers continue to push the boundaries of what is possible.

   - A) looks bright as filmmakers continues to push

   - B) looks bright as filmmakers continuing to push

   - C) looks bright, as filmmakers continue to push

   - D) looks bright as filmmakers push

Passage 13: The importance of education cannot be overstated. Education provides individuals with the knowledge and skills needed to succeed in life. It also promotes critical thinking, creativity, and personal growth. Access to quality education is essential for building a better future for all.

49. The importance of education cannot be overstated.

   - A) can be overstated

   - B) cannot be overstate

- C) cannot be overstating

- D) cannot be overstated

50. Education provides individuals with the knowledge and skills needed to succeed in life.

- A) provides individuals with the knowledge and skill

- B) providing individuals with the knowledge and skills

- C) provide individuals with the knowledge and skills

- D) provides individuals the knowledge and skills

51. It also promotes critical thinking, creativity, and personal growth.

- A) promotes critical thinking, creative, and personal growth

- B) promote critical thinking, creativity, and personal growth

- C) promoting critical thinking, creativity, and personal growth

- D) promoted critical thinking, creativity, and personal growth

52. Access to quality education is essential for building a better future for all.

- A) building a better futures for all

- B) building a better future for everyone

- C) building a better future for all

- D) builds a better future for all

Passage 14: The benefits of reading are well-known. Reading enhances vocabulary, improves concentration, and stimulates the mind. It can also reduce stress and improve empathy. Whether it is fiction or non-fiction, reading can be a valuable and enjoyable pastime.

53. The benefits of reading are well-known.

- A) is well-known

- B) are well-known

- C) is well-known,

- D) is well-knowned

54. Reading enhances vocabulary, improves concentration, and stimulates the mind.

- A) enhances vocabulary
- B) improving concentration, and stimulates
- C) enhancing vocabulary, improves concentration
- D) enhances vocabularies

55. It can also reduce stress and improve empathy.

- A) improve empathies
- B) improves empathy
- C) improve empathy
- D) improving empathy

56. Whether it is fiction or non-fiction, reading can be a valuable and enjoyable pastime.

- A) is fiction or non-fiction,
- B) is fiction or non-fiction;
- C) its fiction or non-fiction,
- D) is fiction or nonfiction

Passage 15: The history of sports is filled with legendary athletes and memorable moments. From the ancient Olympic Games to modern professional sports, athletes have always strived for excellence. Sports bring people together, promote physical fitness, and teach valuable life lessons. The influence of sports on society is undeniable.

57. The history of sports is filled with legendary athletes and memorable moments.

- A) are filled
- B) is filled with legendary athletes, memorable moments
- C) is filled with legendary athlete's and memorable moments
- D) is filled with legendary athletes and memorable moments

58. From the ancient Olympic Games to modern professional sports, athletes have always strived for excellence.

- A) always striving for excellence

- B) always strived for excellence

- C) always strive for excellence

- D) always striven for excellence

59. Sports bring people together, promote physical fitness, and teach valuable life lessons.

- A) brings people together

- B) bring people together, promoting physical fitness

- C) bring people together, promotes physical fitness

- D) bring people together, promote physical fitness

60. The influence of sports on society is undeniable.

- A) influence of sport on society

- B) influence of sports in society

- C) influences of sports on society

- D) influence of sports on societies

Passage 16: The rise of the internet has revolutionized the way we access information. Search engines allow us to find answers to questions in seconds, and online databases provide access to a wealth of knowledge. Social media platforms enable us to connect with people around the world. However, the internet also presents challenges, such as misinformation and privacy concerns.

61. The rise of the internet has revolutionized the way we access information.

- A) revolutionized the way we access informations

- B) revolutionizes the way we access information

- C) revolutionized the ways we access information

- D) has revolutionized the way we access information

62. Search engines allow us to find answers to questions in seconds, and online databases provide access to a wealth of knowledge.

209

- A) provide accesses to a wealth of knowledge

- B) provide access to wealth of knowledge

- C) provides access to a wealth of knowledges

- D) provide access to a wealth of knowledge

63. Social media platforms enable us to connect with people around the world.

- A) enabled us to connect with people

- B) enables us to connect with people

- C) enable us connecting with people

- D) enables us to connect with people

64. However, the internet also presents challenges, such as misinformation and privacy concerns.

- A) such as misinformations and privacy concerns

- B) such as misinformation, and privacy concerns

- C) such as misinformation and privacy concern

- D) such as misinformation and privacy concerns

Passage 17: The history of aviation is a story of innovation and adventure. From the Wright brothers' first flight to modern commercial air travel, aviation has transformed the world. Advances in technology have made air travel safer, faster, and more efficient. The future of aviation promises even more exciting developments.

65. The history of aviation is a story of innovation and adventure.

- A) are a story of innovation and adventure

- B) is a story of innovating and adventure

- C) is a story of innovation and adventuring

- D) is a story of innovation and adventure

66. From the Wright brothers' first flight to modern commercial air travel, aviation has transformed the world.

- A) transforming the world

- B) has transform the world

- C) has transformed world

- D) has transformed the world

67. Advances in technology have made air travel safer, faster, and more efficient.

    - A) made air travel more safer

    - B) has made air travel safer

    - C) making air travel safer

    - D) made air travel safe, faster, and more efficient

68. The future of aviation promises even more exciting developments.

    - A) promises even more excitingly developments

    - B) promise even more exciting developments

    - C) promises even more exciting development

    - D) promises even more exciting developments

Passage 18: The impact of climate change is being felt around the world. Rising temperatures and changing weather patterns are affecting ecosystems and human communities. Efforts to mitigate climate change include reducing greenhouse gas emissions and transitioning to renewable energy sources. Addressing climate change is essential for the health of our planet.

69. The impact of climate change is being felt around the world.

    - A) are being felt around the world

    - B) is felt around the world

    - C) is being felted around the world

    - D) is felted around the world

70. Rising temperatures and changing weather patterns are affecting ecosystems and human communities.

    - A) affecting ecosystems and human community

    - B) affecting ecosystem and human communities

    - C) are affecting ecosystems and human community

    - D) are affecting ecosystems and human communities

71. Efforts to mitigate climate change include reducing greenhouse gas emissions and transitioning to renewable energy sources.

- A) includes reducing greenhouse gas emissions
- B) include reducing greenhouse gas emission
- C) include reducing greenhouse gasses emissions
- D) include reducing greenhouse gas emissions

72. Addressing climate change is essential for the health of our planet.

- A) essential to the health of our planet
- B) essential for the health of planet
- C) essential for the health of our planets
- D) essential for the health of our planet

Passage 19: The benefits of volunteering are numerous. Volunteering provides opportunities to give back to the community, develop new skills, and build meaningful connections. It can also enhance personal growth and improve mental health. Whether it's helping at a local shelter or participating in a community clean-up, volunteering can make a positive impact.

73. The benefits of volunteering are numerous.

- A) is numerous
- B) are numerous.
- C) is numerous.
- D) are numerous

74. Volunteering provides opportunities to give back to the community, develop new skills, and build meaningful connections.

- A) providing opportunities to give back to the community
- B) provides opportunities to give back to the community
- C) providing opportunity to give back to the community
- D) provide opportunities to give back to the community

75. It can also enhance personal growth and improve mental health.

- A) improves

- B) enhancing

- C) improve mental health

- D) improves mental health

Answers

1. **B)** has transformed

2. **D)** has made possible for individuals to stay

3. **D)** allow instant sharing

4. **A)** distraction and a lack of privacy

5. **D)** has significantly evolved

6. **C)** have access

7. **D)** allows for

8. **C)** have explored

9. **C)** fascinating one, filled

10. **C)** over time, they have become more complex

11. **D)** and advanced engineering

12. **D)** form of transportation and recreation around

13. **C)** crucial to the future

14. **D)** reliance on fossil fuels

15. **D)** a clean and sustainable

16. **B)** will continue improving

17. **D)** are well-documented

18. **B)** strengthens

19. **C)** can boost

20. **D)** it's running, swimming, or lifting weights,

21. **D)** expanding rapidly

22. **D)** providing students with access to a wealth of information

23. **D)** offer flexible learning options

24. **D)** remains a significant challenge

25. **D)** is essential for achieving

26. **C)** allows

27. **B)** help to organize one's schedule

28. **D)** stress can be reduced and goals can be accomplished

29. **D)** a wealth of experiences and memories

30. **D)** broadens and enhances

31. **D)** can sometimes be challenging

32. **D)** an opportunity to learn and grow

33. **D)** evokes

34. **B)** brings back memories

35. **D)** a source of motivation and inspiration

36. **D)** many people's lives

37. **D)** fascinates humans for centuries

38. **A)** civilizations used stars

39. **D)** Today, astronomers use

40. **D)** expanded our knowledge of the cosmos

41. **B)** are numerous

42. **D)** provides the essential vitamins and minerals

43. **B)** contribute to overall health and well-being

44. **A)** supports

45. **D)** has rich innovation and creativity

46. **D)** experimented with techniques

47. **D)** revolutionized the industry

48. **D)** looks bright as filmmakers push

49. **D)** cannot be overstated

50. A) provides individuals with the knowledge and skill

51. C) promoting critical thinking, creativity, and personal growth

52. D) builds a better future for all

53. B) are well-known

54. A) enhances vocabulary

55. B) improves empathy

56. D) is fiction or nonfiction

57. D) is filled with legendary athletes and memorable moments

58. B) always strived for excellence

59. D) bring people together, promote physical fitness

60. A) influence of sport on society

61. D) has revolutionized the way we access information

62. C) provides access to a wealth of knowledge

63. D) enables us to connect with people

64. D) such as misinformation and privacy concerns

65. D) is a story of innovation and adventure

66. D) has transformed the world

67. C) making air travel safer

68. D) promises even more exciting developments

69. D) is felted around the world

70. D) are affecting ecosystems and human communities

71. D) include reducing greenhouse gas emissions

72. D) essential for the health of our planet

73. D) are numerous

74. B) provides opportunities to give back to the community

75. A) improves

Section 2: Mathematics (60 Questions in 60 minutes)

1. If $3x + 7 = 19$, what is the value of x?

    - A) 3
    - B) 4
    - C) 5
    - D) 6
    - E) 7

2. What is the value of x in the equation $5x - 3 = 2x + 12$?

    - A) 3
    - B) 4
    - C) 5
    - D) 6
    - E) 7

3. What is the area of a circle with a diameter of 10 units? (Use $\pi \approx 3.14$)

    - A) 25 π
    - B) 50 π
    - C) 75 π
    - D) 100 π
    - E) 78.5

4. If $x^2 - 16 = 0$, what is the value of x?

    - A) 2
    - B) -4, 4
    - C) 4
    - D) -2, 2
    - E) -4

5. What is the slope of the line that passes through the points (1, 2) and (3, 4)?

- A) 1
- B) 2
- C) 3
- D) 4
- E) 5

6. If y = 3x - 1, what is the value of y when x = 5?

    - A) 10
    - B) 11
    - C) 12
    - D) 14
    - E) 15

7. If sqrt (81) = x, what is the value of x?

    - A) 7
    - B) 8
    - C) 9
    - D) 10
    - E) 11

8. What is the perimeter of an equilateral triangle with sides of 6 units each?

    - A) 12
    - B) 18
    - C) 24
    - D) 30
    - E) 36

9. If 3^x = 27, what is the value of x?

    - A) 2
    - B) 3

- C) 4
- D) 5
- E) 6

10. What is the solution to the equation 4x - 5 = 11?

- A) 2
- B) 3
- C) 4
- D) 5
- E) 6

11. What is the circumference of a circle with a diameter of 14 units? (Use π ≈ 3.14)

- A) 22
- B) 28
- C) 44
- D) 48.1
- E) 50

12. If the area of a square is 49 square units, what is the length of one side?

- A) 5
- B) 6
- C) 7
- D) 8
- E) 9

13. What is the value of x in the equation 6x + 2 = 20?

- A) 2
- B) 3
- C) 4
- D) 5

- E) 6

14. What is the area of a triangle with a base of 12 units and a height of 8 units?

    - A) 24

    - B) 36

    - C) 48

    - D) 60

    - E) 96

15. If $y = 4x + 6$, what is the value of y when $x = 3$?

    - A) 15

    - B) 16

    - C) 17

    - D) 18

    - E) 19

16. What is the volume of a cube with an edge length of 4 units?

    - A) 24

    - B) 32

    - C) 48

    - D) 64

    - E) 80

17. What is the solution to the equation $5x + 4 = 24$?

    - A) 3

    - B) 4

    - C) 5

    - D) 6

    - E) 7

18. If $4x - 7 = 17$, what is the value of x?

- A) 5

- B) 6

- C) 7

- D) 8

- E) 9

19. If the perimeter of a rectangle is 30 units and its length is 10 units, what is the width?

- A) 2

- B) 3

- C) 4

- D) 5

- E) 6

20. What is the value of x in the equation $x^2 = 49$?

- A) 5

- B) 6

- C) 7

- D) 8

- E) 9

21. If $y = x^2 + 4x + 4$, what is the value of y when x = 2?

- A) 12

- B) 14

- C) 16

- D) 18

- E) 20

22. What is the slope of the line $y = 5x + 3$?

- A) 1

- B) 2
- C) 3
- D) 4
- E) 5

23. If 7x - 3 = 18, what is the value of x?

  - A) 2
  - B) 3
  - C) 4
  - D) 5
  - E) 6

24. What is the area of a rectangle with a length of 14 units and a width of 3 units?

  - A) 24
  - B) 30
  - C) 36
  - D) 42
  - E) 48

25. If 9x + 6 = 42, what is the value of x?

  - A) 3
  - B) 4
  - C) 5
  - D) 6
  - E) 7

26. What is the volume of a cylinder with a radius of 3 units and a height of 7 units? (Use $\pi \approx 3.14$)

  - A) 65.56
  - B) 71.38

- C) 84.54

- D) 113.04

- E) 197.82

27. If $x^2 - 25 = 0$, what is the value of x?

    - A) 5

    - B) -5, 5

    - C) -5

    - D) 0.5

    - E) 0, -5

28. What is the value of x in the equation $2x - 3 = 11$?

    - A) 4

    - B) 5

    - C) 6

    - D) 7

    - E) 8

29. What is the value of x in the equation $x^2 - 9 = 0$?

    - A) 3

    - B) -3, 3

    - C) -3

    - D) 0, 3

    - E) 0, -3

30. If the perimeter of a triangle is 36 units and two of its sides measure 12 units each, how long is the third side?

    - A) 10

    - B) 12

    - C) 14

- D) 16

- E) 18

31. What is the slope of the line that passes through the points (3, 4) and (6, 10)?

  - A) 1

  - B) 2

  - C) 3

  - D) 4

  - E) 5

32. If y = 5x + 4, what is the value of y when x = 4?

  - A) 18

  - B) 19

  - C) 20

  - D) 22

  - E) 24

33. What is the value of x in the equation 7x - 4 = 24?

  - A) 3

  - B) 4

  - C) 5

  - D) 6

  - E) 7

34. What is the area of a triangle with a base of 16 units and a height of 5 units?

  - A) 30

  - B) 40

  - C) 50

  - D) 60

  - E) 70

35. What is the value of x in the equation $x^2 + 6x + 8 = 0$?

- A) -2, -4

- B) -4, 4

- C) -2, 2

- D) 2, -4

- E) 4, -2

36. If the area of a circle is 49π square units, what is the radius of the circle? (Use π ≈ 3.14)

- A) 5

- B) 6

- C) 7

- D) 8

- E) 9

37. What is the volume of a cube with an edge length of 6 units?

- A) 36

- B) 72

- C) 108

- D) 216

- E) 324

38. If $8x + 3 = 35$, what is the value of x?

- A) 3

- B) 4

- C) 5

- D) 6

- E) 7

39. What is the value of x in the equation $9x - 5 = 22$?

- A) 3
- B) 4
- C) 5
- D) 6
- E) 7

40. What is the solution to the equation x^2 - 49 = 0?

- A) -7, 7
- B) 0.7
- C) 7
- D) -7, 0
- E) 0, -7

41. What is the perimeter of a square with a side length of 10 units?

- A) 30
- B) 40
- C) 50
- D) 60
- E) 70

42. What is the slope of the line y = 2x + 7?

- A) 1
- B) 2
- C) 3
- D) 4
- E) 5

43. If 6x - 4 = 20, what is the value of x?

- A) 3
- B) 4

- C) 5
- D) 6
- E) 7

44. What is the value of x in the equation $5x + 8 = 23$?

    - A) 2
    - B) 3
    - C) 4
    - D) 5
    - E) 6

45. If the area of a triangle is 24 square units and its base measures 6 units, what is the height of the triangle?

    - A) 6
    - B) 7
    - C) 8
    - D) 9
    - E) 10

46. What is the volume of a cylinder with a radius of 4 units and a height of 5 units? (Use $\pi \approx 3.14$)

    - A) 40π
    - B) 50π
    - C) 60π
    - D) 70π
    - E) 80π

47. If $x^2 - 1 = 0$, what is the value of x?

    - A) -1, 1
    - B) 0, 1
    - C) -1

- D) 0, -1

- E) 1, -1

48. What is the value of x in the equation $4x + 5 = 29$?

   - A) 5

   - B) 6

   - C) 7

   - D) 8

   - E) 9

49. What is the area of a rectangle with a length of 9 units and a width of 7 units?

   - A) 56

   - B) 57

   - C) 58

   - D) 63

   - E) 65

50. If $3x + 2 = 17$, what is the value of x?

   - A) 4

   - B) 5

   - C) 6

   - D) 7

   - E) 8

51. What is the value of x in the equation $x^2 - 36 = 0$?

   - A) 6

   - B) -6, 6

   - C) -6

   - D) 0.6

- E) 0, -6

52. If the perimeter of a triangle is 40 units and two of its sides, measuring 15 units each, how long is the third side?

- A) 10
- B) 15
- C) 20
- D) 25
- E) 30

53. What is the value of x in the equation 5x + 3 = 28?

- A) 4
- B) 5
- C) 6
- D) 7
- E) 8

54. What is the area of a circle with a radius of 8 units? (Use $\pi \approx 3.14$)

- A) 64 π
- B) 128 π
- C) 256 π
- D) 100.48
- E) 201.06

55. If y = x^2 + 3x + 2, what is the value of y when x = 4?

- A) 22
- B) 24
- C) 26
- D) 28
- E) 30

56. What is the slope of the line that passes through the points (2, 3) and (4, 9)?

- A) 2
- B) 3
- C) 4
- D) 5
- E) 6

57. If $4x + 7 = 31$, what is the value of x?

- A) 4
- B) 5
- C) 6
- D) 7
- E) 8

58. What is the value of x in the equation $5x - 4 = 21$?

- A) 4
- B) 5
- C) 6
- D) 7
- E) 8

59. What is the volume of a cube with an edge length of 7 units?

- A) 49
- B) 98
- C) 147
- D) 196
- E) 343

60. What is the value of x in the equation $x^2 + 4x - 12 = 0$?

- A) -6, 2
- B) -4, 3
- C) -3, 4
- D) 2, -6
- E) 4, -3

Answers

1. B) 4

Subtracting 7 from both sides gives 3x = 12. Dividing 12 by 3 gives x = 4.

2. C) 5

Subtracting 2x and adding 3 to both sides gives 3x = 15. Dividing 15 by 3 gives x = 5.

3. E) 78.5

The radius is 5 units. The area of a circle is πr^2 = 3.14 * 5^2 = 78.5.

4. B) -4, 4

x^2 - 16 = 0 is factored as (x - 4) (x + 4) = 0, therefore x = 4 and x = -4.

5. A) 1

The slope m = (y2 - y1) / (x2 - x1) = (4 - 2) / (3 - 1) = 2 / 2 = 1.

6. D) 14

Substituting x = 5 into y = 3x - 1 gives y = 3(5) - 1 = 15 - 1 = 14.

7. C) 9

The square root of 81 is 9.

8. B) 18

The perimeter of an equilateral triangle is 3 * side = 3 * 6 = 18.

9. B) 3

3^3 = 27, therefore x = 3.

10. C) 4

Adding 5 to both sides gives 4x = 16. Dividing 16 by 4 gives x = 4.

11. C) 44

The circumference of a circle is πd = 3.14 * 14 ≈ 44.

12. C) 7

If the area is 49, the length of one side is sqrt (49) = 7.

13. B) 3

Subtracting 2 from both sides gives 6x = 18. Dividing 18 by 6 gives x = 3.

14. C) 48

The area of a triangle is 1/2 * base * height = 1/2 * 12 * 8 = 48.

15. D) 18

Substituting x = 3 into y = 4x + 6 gives y = 4(3) + 6 = 12 + 6 = 18.

16. D) 64

The volume of a cube is side^3 = 4^3 = 64.

17. B) 4

Subtracting 4 from both sides gives 5x = 20. Dividing 20 by 5 gives x = 4.

18. B) 6

Adding 7 to both sides gives 4x = 24. Dividing 24 by 4 gives x = 6.

19. D) 5

The perimeter of a rectangle is 2 (length + width). Dividing 30 by 2 gives 15, and subtracting 10 from 15 gives width = 5.

20. C) 7

The square root of 49 is 7.

21. C) 16

Substituting x = 2 into y = x^2 + 4x + 4 gives y = 2^2 + 4(2) + 4 = 4 + 8 + 4 = 16.

22. E) 5

The slope of the line is the coefficient of x at y = 5x + 3.

23. B) 3

Adding 3 to both sides gives 7x = 21. Dividing 21 by 7 gives x = 3.

24. D) 42

The area of a rectangle is length * width = 14 * 3 = 42.

25. B) 4

Subtracting 6 from both sides gives 9x = 36. Dividing 36 by 9 gives x = 4.

26. E) 197.82

The volume of a cylinder is πr^2h = 3.14 * 3^2 * 7 = 3.14 * 9 * 7 = 198.34.

27. B) -5, 5

x^2 - 25 = 0 is factored as (x - 5) (x + 5) = 0, therefore x = 5 and x = -5.

28. D) 7

Adding 3 to both sides gives 2x = 14. Dividing 14 by 2 gives x = 7.

29. B) -3, 3

x^2 - 9 = 0 is factored as (x - 3) (x + 3) = 0, therefore x = 3 and x = -3.

30. B) 12

The perimeter of a triangle is the sum of its sides. Subtracting 24 from 36 gives the third side = 12.

31. B) 2

The slope m = (y2 - y1) / (x2 - x1) = (10 - 4) / (6 - 3) = 6 / 3 = 2.

32. E) 24

Substituting x = 4 into y = 5x + 4 gives y = 5(4) + 4 = 20 + 4 = 24.

33. B) 4

Adding 4 to both sides gives 7x = 28. Dividing 28 by 7 gives x = 4.

34. B) 40

The area of a triangle is 1/2 * base * height = 1/2 * 16 * 5 = 40.

35. A) -2, -4

x^2 + 6x + 8 = 0 is factored as (x + 2) (x + 4) = 0, therefore x = -2 and x = -4.

36. C) 7

The area of a circle is πr^2. If the area is 49π, then r^2 = 49, the square root of 49 is 7.

37. D) 216

The volume of a cube is side^3 = 6^3 = 216.

38. B) 4

Subtracting 3 from both sides gives 8x = 32. Dividing 32 by 8 gives x = 4.

39. A) 3

Adding 5 to both sides gives 9x = 27. Dividing 27 by 9 gives x = 3.

40. A) -7, 7

The equation x^2 - 49 = 0 is factored as (x - 7) (x + 7) = 0, therefore x = 7 and x = -7.

41. B) 40

The perimeter of a square is 4 * side and the side measures 10, then 4 * 10 = 40.

42. B) 2

The slope of the line is the coefficient of x at y = 2x + 7.

43. B) 4

Adding 4 to both sides gives 6x = 24. Dividing 24 by 6 gives x = 4.

44. B) 3

Subtracting 8 from both sides gives 5x = 15. Dividing 15 by 5 gives x = 3.

45. C) 8

The area of a triangle is 1/2 * base * height. If the area is 24 and the base is 6, then 1/2 * 6 * height = 24. Solving gives height = 8.

46. E) 80π

The volume of a cylinder is πr^2h = 3.14 * 4^2 * 5 = 3.14 * 16 * 5 = 251.2.

47. A) -1, 1

The equation x^2 - 1 = 0 is factored as (x - 1) (x + 1) = 0, therefore x = 1 and x = -1.

48. B) 6

Subtracting 5 from both sides gives 4x = 24. Dividing 24 by 4 gives x = 6.

49. D) 63

The area of a rectangle is length * width = 9 * 7 = 63.

50. B) 5

Subtracting 2 from both sides gives $3x = 15$. Dividing 15 by 3 gives $x = 5$.

51. B) -6, 6

The equation $x^2 - 36 = 0$ is factored as $(x - 6)(x + 6) = 0$, therefore $x = 6$ and $x = -6$.

52. A) 10

The perimeter of a triangle is the sum of its sides. If two sides measure 15 units each, then the third side is $40 - 30 = 10$.

53. B) 5

Subtracting 3 from both sides gives $5x = 25$. Dividing 25 by 5 gives $x = 5$.

54. E) 201.06

The area of a circle is $\pi r^2 = 3.14 * 8^2 = 3.14 * 64 = 201.06$.

55. E) 30

Substituting $x = 4$ into $y = x^2 + 3x + 2$ gives $y = 4^2 + 3(4) + 2 = 16 + 12 + 2 = 30$.

56. B) 3

The slope $m = (y2 - y1) / (x2 - x1) = (9 - 3) / (4 - 2) = 6 / 2 = 3$.

57. C) 6

Subtracting 7 from both sides gives $4x = 24$. Dividing 24 by 4 gives $x = 6$.

58. B) 5

Adding 4 to both sides gives $5x = 25$. Dividing 25 by 5 gives $x = 5$.

59. E) 343

The volume of a cube is $side^3 = 7^3 = 343$.

60. A) -6, 2

The equation $x^2 + 4x - 12 = 0$ is factored as $(x + 6)(x - 2) = 0$, therefore $x = -6$ and $x = 2$.

Section 3: Reading (40 Questions in 35 minutes)

Passage 1: The small mountain town was covered in snow. The chimneys of the houses billowed smoke and the sound of crackling wood could be heard in the cold air. The children played in the snow, making snowmen and throwing snowballs at each other.

1. What covered the small mountain town?

    - A) Leaves

    - B) Sand

    - C) Snow

    - D) Flowers

2. What was heard in the cold air of the town?

    - A) The singing of birds

    - B) The sound of the sea

    - C) The crackling of wood

    - D) The traffic noise

3. What were the children doing in the snow?

    - A) They read books

    - B) They made snowmen and threw snowballs

    - C) They swam

    - D) They painted pictures

Passage 2: The market was full of colors and aromas. Fresh fruits glistened in the sun, and vendors offered samples to buyers. The flower stalls added a touch of color and fragrance to the environment.

4. What did the sellers offer to the buyers in the market?

    - A) Discounts

    - B) Samples

    - C) Bags

    - D) Drinks

5. What did the flower stalls add to the market atmosphere?

    - A) Music

- B) Fragrance and color

- C) Noises

- D) Chairs

6. What was shining under the sun in the market?

   - A) The fresh fruits

   - B) The toys

   - C) The lamps

   - D) The chairs

Passage 3: The desert seemed endless. The sand dunes stretched as far as the eye could see, and the sun burned in the clear sky. The wind raised clouds of dust that danced in the hot air.

7. What stretched as far as the eye could see in the desert?

   - A) The mountains

   - B) The sand dunes

   - C) The trees

   - D) The lakes

8. What was the sky like in the desert?

   - A) Cloudy

   - B) Clear

   - C) Rainy

   - D) Dark

9. What did the wind raise in the desert?

   - A) Leaves

   - B) Water

   - C) Dust clouds

   - D) Rocks

Passage 4: The central square of the town was a meeting place. Water fountains gurgled happily, and families gathered to enjoy the day. The children ran and played while the adults talked.

10. What did the water fountains do in the central plaza?

- A) They shone

- B) They gurgled with joy

- C) They were off

- D) They were dirty

11. What were the children doing in the central square?

- A) They studied

- B) They ran and played

- C) They slept

- D) They worked

12. What were the adults doing in the central square?

- A) They sang

- B) They painted

- C) They were talking

- D) They cooked

Passage 5: The dock was bustling with activity. Boats arrived and departed, and fishermen unloaded their catch of the day. The seagulls were flying over the water, hoping to get some food.

13. What were the fishermen doing on the dock?

- A) They sold fish

- B) They unloaded their catch of the day

- C) They repaired ships

- D) They bought networks

14. What did the seagulls hope to achieve?

- A) Nests

- B) Networks

- C) Food

- D) Shelter

15. What best describes the activity on the dock?

- A) Quiet

- B) Slow

- C) Full of activity

- D) Deserted

Passage 6: The national park was a natural refuge. The paths were surrounded by tall trees, and the rivers ran clear and cool. Visitors could observe wildlife in their natural habitat.

16. What surrounded the trails in the national park?

- A) Shrubs

- B) Flowers

- C) Tall trees

- D) Rocks

17. How did the rivers flow in the national park?

- A) Slow and warm

- B) Clear and fresh

- C) Dirty and stagnant

- D) Dark and fast

18. What could visitors see in the national park?

- A) Old buildings

- B) Domestic animals

- C) Wildlife

- D) Campers

Passage 7: The community library was a place of learning and discovery. The shelves were filled with books, and computers were available for everyone to use. Activities for children included story reading and crafts.

19. What was full of books in the community library?

- A) The tables
- B) The shelves
- C) The desks
- D) The chairs

20. What were the computers available for in the community library?

- A) For sale
- B) For the use of all
- C) For decoration
- D) For games

21. What activities for children are mentioned in the passage?

- A) Board games
- B) Reading stories and crafts
- C) Music classes
- D) Sports

Passage 8: The restaurant at the top of the hill offered a stunning view of the valley. The outdoor tables allowed diners to enjoy the scenery while savoring their meals. The cool breeze made the experience even more pleasant.

22. What offered a stunning view of the valley?

- A) The garden
- B) The restaurant at the top of the hill
- C) The market
- D) The central square

23. What did outdoor tables allow diners?

- A) Eat quickly

- B) Rest

- C) Enjoy the landscape

- D) Read books

24. What was the cool breeze doing in the restaurant?

- A) It cooled the food

- B) It made the experience more pleasant

- C) It brought dust

- D) It moved the chairs

Passage 9: The zoo was full of visitors. The children looked at the animals fascinated, and the parents took photos. The lions slept in the shade, while the monkeys jumped from one tree to another.

25. What were the children doing at the zoo?

- A) They bought souvenirs

- B) They looked at the animals fascinated

- C) They ate ice cream

- D) They slept

26. What were the parents doing at the zoo?

- A) They read books

- B) They took photos

- C) They painted pictures

- D) They fed the animals

27. What were the monkeys doing in the zoo?

- A) They slept under the shade

- B) They jumped from one tree to another

- C) They swam in the lake

- D) They ran on the ground

Passage 10: The beach was full of life. The waves crashed gently on the shore, and people swam and played in the water. Street vendors offered cold drinks and snacks to bathers.

28. How did the waves break on the shore?

   - A) Strong

   - B) Gently

   - C) Fast

   - D) Slow

29. What were people doing in the water?

   - A) They fished

   - B) They played and swam

   - C) They sailed

   - D) They painted

30. What did the street vendors on the beach offer?

   - A) Clothing

   - B) Cold drinks and snacks

   - C) Toys

   - D) Books

Passage 11: The mall was decorated for the holidays. Lights shone on every corner, and the shop windows were filled with Christmas products. People walked around, enjoying the festive atmosphere.

31. How was the shopping center decorated?

   - A) With lights

   - B) With flowers

   - C) With balloons

   - D) With posters

32. What filled the windows of the shopping center?

   - A) Summer clothes

- B) Christmas products

- C) Electronics

- D) Toys

33. How did the people in the mall feel?

- A) Sad

- B) Festive

- C) Tired

- D) Angry

Passage 12: The river meandered peacefully through the valley. The fishermen stood on its banks, waiting patiently for the fish to take the bait. The trees along the river provided cooling shade.

34. How did the river wind through the valley?

- A) Quickly

- B) With peace of mind

- C) With violence

- D) With danger

35. What did the fishermen do on the banks of the river?

- A) They swam

- B) They waited patiently for the fish to take the bait

- C) They planted trees

- D) They built houses

36. What did the trees along the river provide?

- A) Fruits

- B) Wood

- C) Cooling shade

- D) Flowers

Passage 13: The plane took off smoothly, rising above the clouds. Passengers looked out the windows, marveling at the view. The flight attendants offered drinks and snacks while the pilots announced the altitude.

37. How did the plane take off?

- A) Very quickly

- B) Gently

- C) Abruptly

- D) Very slowly

38. What did the flight attendants offer to the passengers?

- A) Books and magazines

- B) Toys

- C) Drinks and snacks

- D) Clothing

39. What were the pilots announcing?

- A) The destination

- B) The altitude

- C) The speed

- D) The arrival time

Passage 14: The community garden was in full harvest. People picked fresh vegetables and ripe fruits. The air was filled with sweet aromas and the sounds of laughter and conversation.

40. What did people do in the community garden?

- A) They planted seeds

- B) They collected fresh vegetables and ripe fruits

- C) They watered the plants

- D) They harvested flowers

Answers

1. C) Snow

The passage mentions that the small mountain town was covered in snow.

2. C) The crackling of wood

The passage says that the sound of crackling wood could be heard in the cold air.

3. B) They made dolls and threw snowballs

The passage mentions that children played in the snow making dolls and throwing snowballs at each other.

4. B) Samples

The passage mentions that sellers offered samples to buyers.

5. B) Fragrance and color

The passage says that the flower stalls added a touch of color and fragrance to the environment.

6. A) Fresh fruits

The passage mentions that the fresh fruits shone under the sun.

7. B) Sand dunes

The passage mentions that the sand dunes stretched as far as the eye could see.

8. B) Clear

The passage says that the sun was burning in the clear sky.

9. C) Dust clouds

The passage mentions that the wind raised clouds of dust.

10. B) They gurgled with joy

The passage mentions that the water fountains gurgled with joy.

11. B) They ran and played

The passage mentions that children ran and played in the central square.

12. C) They talked

The passage says that the adults were talking.

13. B) They unloaded their catch of the day

The passage mentions that fishermen unloaded their catch of the day at the dock.

14. C) Food

The passage says that the seagulls were hoping to get some food.

15. C) Full of activity

The passage mentions that the dock was bustling with activity.

16. C) Tall trees

The passage mentions that the paths were surrounded by tall trees.

17. B) Clear and fresh

The passage mentions that the rivers ran clear and cool.

18. C) Wildlife

The passage says that visitors could observe wildlife in their natural habitat.

19. B) The shelves

The passage mentions that the shelves were full of books.

20. B) For the use of all

The passage says that computers were available for everyone to use.

21. B) Reading stories and crafts

The passage mentions that children's activities included story reading and crafts.

22. B) The restaurant at the top of the hill

The passage mentions that the restaurant at the top of the hill offered a stunning view of the valley.

23. C) Enjoy the landscape

The passage says that the outdoor tables allowed diners to enjoy the scenery.

24. B) It made the experience more pleasant

The passage mentions that the cool breeze made the experience even more pleasant.

25. B) They looked at the animals fascinated

The passage says that the children looked fascinated at the animals in the zoo.

26. B) They took photos

The passage mentions that the parents took photos.

27. B) They jumped from one tree to another

The passage says that the monkeys jumped from one tree to another.

28. B) Gently

The passage mentions that the waves broke gently on the shore.

29. B) They played and swam

The passage says that people played and swam in the water.

30. B) Cold drinks and snacks

The passage mentions that street vendors offered cold drinks and snacks.

31. A) With lights

The passage mentions that the shopping center was decorated with lights.

32. B) Christmas products

The passage says that the shop windows were full of Christmas products.

33. B) Festive

The passage mentions that people enjoyed the festive atmosphere.

34. B) With peace of mind

The passage mentions that the river meandered peacefully through the valley.

35. B) They waited patiently for the fish to take the bait

The passage mentions that the fishermen stood on the banks of the river waiting patiently for the fish to take the bait.

36. C) Refreshing shadow

The passage says that the trees along the river provided cooling shade.

37. B) Gently

The passage mentions that the plane took off smoothly.

38. C) Drinks and snacks

The passage says that the flight attendants offered drinks and snacks to the passengers.

39. B) Altitude

The passage mentions that the pilots announced the altitude.

40. B) They collected fresh vegetables and ripe fruits

The passage says that the people in the community garden gathered fresh vegetables and ripe fruits.

Section 4: Science (40 Questions in 35 minutes)

Passage 1: A group of scientists investigated the effect of different types of nutrient solutions on the growth of a type of fungus. The scientists prepared four groups of mushrooms: Group A received a glucose-based solution, Group B received a starch-based solution, Group C received a fructose-based solution, and Group D received no solution. After 8 weeks, the mushroom mass was measured.

Results Table:

Cluster	Average Mass (oz)
Group A	0.3527 oz
Group B	0.4233 oz
Group C	0.5291 oz
Group D	0.1764 oz

1. Which group of mushrooms grew the most in mass?

   - A) Group A

   - B) Group B

   - C) Group C

   - D) Group D

2. What is the difference in mass between Group A and Group D?

   - A) 0.1764 oz

   - B) 0.2469 oz

   - C) 0.3527 oz

   - D) 0.5291 oz

3. What variable was manipulated in the experiment?

   - A) The type of fungus

   - B) The type of nutrient solution

- C) The amount of water

- D) The temperature

Passage 2: The effect of pressure on the boiling of a liquid was investigated. Experiments were carried out at different pressures and the boiling point of liquid was measured.

Results Table:

Pressure (atm)	Boiling Point of Liquid (°F)
0.5	140°F
1	176°F
1.5	212°F
2	248°F

4. What pressure showed the highest boiling point of the liquid?

- A) 0.5 atm

- B) 1 atm

- C) 1.5 atm

- D) 2 atm

5. How does pressure affect the boiling point of a liquid?

- A) It decreases it

- B) It increases it

- C) It keeps it constant

- D) It has no effect

6. If the pressure increases from 1 atm to 1.5 atm, by how much does the boiling point increase?

- A) 50°F

- B) 68°F

- C) 86°F

- D) 104°F

Passage 3: An experiment was conducted to observe the effect of sugar concentration on fermentation. Three solutions with different sugar concentrations were used: low, medium, and high. The amount of carbon dioxide produced during fermentation was measured.

Results Table:

Sugar Concentration	CO2 Produced (g)
Low	5
Medium	15
High	25

7. Which concentration of sugar produced the most carbon dioxide?

- A) Low
- B) Medium
- C) High
- D) They all produced the same

8. How does sugar concentration affect carbon dioxide production?

- A) It decreases
- B) It increases
- C) It keeps it constant
- D) It has no effect

9. What variable was measured in the experiment?

- A) The sugar concentration
- B) The type of solution
- C) The amount of carbon dioxide produced
- D) The fermentation time

Passage 4: The relationship between water salinity and the density of a type of shrimp was studied. Four water samples were prepared with different salinity levels:

0%, 1%, 2% and 3%. The density of shrimp in each sample was measured after 4 weeks.

Results Table:

Salinity Level (%)	Shrimp Density (lb/in³)
0	0.0361 lb/in³
1	0.0397 lb/in³
2	0.0434 lb/in³
3	0.0470 lb/in³

10. What level of salinity resulted in the highest density of the shrimp?

- A) 0%
- B) 1%
- C) 2%
- D) 3%

11. What variable was manipulated in the experiment?

- A) The type of shrimp
- B) The salinity of the water
- C) The amount of water
- D) The temperature

12. How does water salinity affect shrimp density?

- A) It decreases
- B) It increases
- C) It keeps it constant
- D) It has no effect

Passage 5: A study analyzed the relationship between the time of exposure to sunlight and vitamin D production in the skin. Different groups of people were exposed to sunlight for 15, 30, 45 and 60 minutes. The amount of vitamin D produced was measured.

Results Table:

Exposure Time (minutes)	Vitamin D Production (ng/ml)
15	10
30	20
45	30
60	40

13. How long of exposure resulted in the greatest production of vitamin D?

- A) 15 minutes

- B) 30 minutes

- C) 45 minutes

- D) 60 minutes

14. How does the time of exposure to sunlight affect the production of vitamin D?

- A) It decreases

- B) It increases

- C) It keeps it constant

- D) It has no effect

15. What variable was measured in the study?

- A) The number of people

- B) The exposure time

- C) The amount of vitamin D produced

- D) The age of the people

Passage 6: An experiment was conducted to investigate the effect of temperature on the solubility of salt in water. The amount of salt dissolved in 100 ml of water at different temperatures was measured.

Results Table:

Temperature (°F)	Salt Solubility (g/100 ml)
50	20
68	30
86	40
104	50

16. What temperature showed the greatest solubility of the salt?

- A) 50°F
- B) 68°F
- C) 86°F
- D) 104°F

17. How does temperature affect the solubility of salt in water?

- A) It decreases
- B) It increases
- C) It keeps it constant
- D) It has no effect

18. What variable was manipulated in the experiment?

- A) The amount of water
- B) The temperature
- C) The pressure
- D) The volume of salt

Passage 7: A study analyzed the relationship between the amount of physical exercise and resting heart rate. A group of people were surveyed and their weekly exercise amount and resting heart rate were recorded.

Results Table:

Weekly Exercise Amount (hours)	Resting Heart Rate (bpm)
0	80
1–2	75
3–4	70
5–6	65

19. How many hours of weekly exercise were associated with the lowest resting heart rate?

- A) 0 hours

- B) 1–2 hours

- C) 3–4 hours

- D) 5–6 hours

20. How does the amount of physical exercise affect resting heart rate?

- A) It increases it

- B) It decreases it

- C) It keeps it constant

- D) It has no effect

21. What variable was measured in the study?

- A) The number of people

- B) The amount of physical exercise

- C) The heart rate at rest

- D) The age of the people

Passage 8: The relationship between the oxygen concentration in the water and the metabolic activity of the fish was investigated. The fish were exposed to different oxygen concentrations and their metabolic rate was measured.

Results Table:

Oxygen Concentration (ppm)	Metabolic Rate (kcal/day)
5 ppm	0.024 kcal/day
10 ppm	0.036 kcal/day
15 ppm	0.048 kcal/day
20 ppm	0.060 kcal/day

22. What oxygen concentration resulted in the highest metabolic rate?

- A) 5 ppm

- B) 10 ppm

- C) 15 ppm

- D) 20 ppm

23. How does oxygen concentration affect metabolic rate?

- A) It decreases

- B) It increases

- C) It keeps it constant

- D) It has no effect

24. What variable was measured in the experiment?

- A) The number of fish

- B) The oxygen concentration

- C) The metabolic rate

- D) The type of fish

Passage 9: An experiment was conducted to study the effect of sodium chloride concentration on the boiling of water. Four solutions with different concentrations of sodium chloride were used: 0%, 2%, 4% and 6%. The boiling point of each solution was measured.

Results Table:

Sodium Chloride Concentration (%)	Boiling Point (°F)
0	212
2	215.6
4	219.2
6	222.8

25. What concentration of sodium chloride resulted in the highest boiling point?

- A) 0%

- B) 2%

- C) 4%

- D) 6%

26. How does the concentration of sodium chloride affect the boiling point of water?

- A) It decreases

- B) It increases

- C) It keeps it constant

- D) It has no effect

27. What variable was measured in the experiment?

- A) The amount of water

- B) The temperature

- C) The concentration of sodium chloride

- D) The boiling time

Passage 10: An experiment was conducted to study the effect of different sound frequencies on seed germination. Three groups of seeds were exposed to different sound frequencies: low, medium, and high. The germination rate was measured after 10 days

Results Table:

Sound Frequency	Germination Rate (%)
Low	40
Medium	60
High	80

28. What sound frequency resulted in the highest germination rate?

- A) Low Frequency
- B) Medium Frequency
- C) High Frequency
- D) They were all the same

29. How does sound frequency affect the germination rate?

- A) It decreases
- B) It increases
- C) It keeps it constant
- D) It has no effect

30. What variable was manipulated in the experiment?

- A) The type of seeds
- B) The amount of water
- C) The frequency of sound
- D) Exposure time

Passage 11: The relationship between the amount of sugar in a solution and the viscosity of the solution was investigated. Solutions with different sugar concentrations were prepared and their viscosity was measured.

Results Table:

Sugar Concentration (%)	Viscosity (cps)
0	1
5	2
10	3
15	4

31. What concentration of sugar resulted in the greatest viscosity?

- A) 0%
- B) 5%
- C) 10%
- D) 15%

32. How does the amount of sugar affect the viscosity of the solution?

- A) It decreases
- B) It increases
- C) It keeps it constant
- D) It has no effect

33. What variable was measured in the experiment?

- A) The amount of solution
- B) The temperature
- C) The viscosity of the solution
- D) The sugar concentration

Passage 12: A study analyzed the effect of different concentrations of chlorine on the purity of pool water. Water samples were prepared with different concentrations of chlorine and the amount of bacteria present was measured after 24 hours.

Results Table:

Chlorine Concentration (ppm)	Bacteria Count (CFU/ml)
0	1000
1	200
2	50
3	10

34. What concentration of chlorine resulted in the fewest bacteria?

- A) 0 ppm

- B) 1 ppm

- C) 2 ppm

- D) 3 ppm

35. How does the concentration of chlorine affect the number of bacteria in the water?

- A) It decreases

- B) It increases

- C) It keeps it constant

- D) It has no effect

36. What variable was manipulated in the experiment?

- A) The amount of water

- B) The chlorine concentration

- C) The water temperature

- D) The exposure time

Passage 13: An experiment was carried out to analyze the effect of the type of surface on the rate of decomposition of organic matter. Samples of organic matter were placed on different surfaces: sand, earth, and rock. The decomposition rate was measured after 30 days.

Results Table:

Surface Type	Decomposition Rate (%)
Sand	10
Earth	25
Rock	5

37. What type of surface resulted in the highest rate of decomposition?

- A) Sand

- B) Earth

- C) Rock

- D) They were all the same

38. How does the type of surface affect the rate of decomposition of organic matter?

- A) It decreases

- B) It increases

- C) It keeps it constant

- D) It has no effect

39. What variable was manipulated in the experiment?

- A) The amount of organic matter

- B) The temperature

- C) The type of surface

- D) The exposure time

Passage 14: A study investigated the effect of the amount of water on biomass production in algae. Algae samples were prepared with different volumes of water and the biomass produced was measured after 2 weeks.

Results Table:

Water Volume (gal)	Biomass Produced (oz)
0.0264 gal	0.1764 oz
0.0528 gal	0.3527 oz
0.0791 gal	0.5291 oz
0.1057 gal	0.7055 oz

40. How much volume of water resulted in the greatest biomass production?

- A) 0.0264 gal

- B) 0.0528 gal

- C) 0.0791 gal

- D) 0.1057 gal

Answers

1. C) Group C

Group C, which received a fructose-based solution, had the highest mass of 0.5291 oz.

2. B) 0.1764 oz

The difference in mass between Group A (0.3527 oz) and Group D (0.1764 oz) is 0.1764 oz.

3. B) The type of nutrient solution

The variable manipulated in the experiment was the type of nutrient solution.

4. D) 2 atm

At 2 atm, the boiling point of the liquid is 248°F, the highest recorded.

5. B) Increases it

As the pressure increases, the boiling point of the liquid also increases.

6. B) 68°F

It increases from 176°F to 212°F when the pressure goes from 1 atm to 1.5 atm.

7. C) High

The high sugar concentration produced the greatest amount of carbon dioxide (25 g CO_2).

8. B) It increases

As sugar concentration increases, so does carbon dioxide production.

9. C) The amount of carbon dioxide produced

The variable measured in the experiment was the amount of carbon dioxide produced.

10. D) 3%

The 3% salinity level resulted in the highest shrimp density (0.0470 lb/in³).

11. B) The salinity of the water

The variable manipulated in the experiment was the salinity of the water.

12. B) It increases

As the salinity of the water increases, the density of the shrimp also increases.

13. D) 60 minutes

60 minutes of sunlight exposure resulted in the highest production of vitamin D (40 ng/ml).

14. B) It increases

As the exposure time to sunlight increases, so does the production of vitamin D.

15. C) The amount of vitamin D produced

The variable measured in the study was the amount of vitamin D produced.

16. D) 104°F

The temperature of 104°F showed the highest solubility of the salt (50 g/100 ml).

17. B) It increases

As the temperature increases, the solubility of the salt also increases.

18. B) Temperature

The variable manipulated in the experiment was temperature.

19. D) 5–6 hours

5–6 hours of weekly exercise was associated with the lowest resting heart rate (65 bpm).

20. B) It decreases it

As the amount of physical exercise increases, resting heart rate decreases.

21. C) Heart rate at rest

The variable measured in the study was resting heart rate.

22. D) 20 ppm

The concentration of 20 ppm oxygen resulted in the highest metabolic rate (0.060 kcal/day).

23. B) It increases

As oxygen concentration increases, so does metabolic rate.

24. C) Metabolic rate

The variable measured in the experiment was the metabolic rate.

25. D) 6%

The sodium chloride concentration of 6% resulted in the highest boiling point (222.8°F).

26. B) It increases

As the concentration of sodium chloride increases, the boiling point of water also increases.

27. C) The concentration of sodium chloride

The variable measured in the experiment was the concentration of sodium chloride.

28. C) High Frequency

The high frequency resulted in the highest germination rate (80%).

29. B) It increases

As the sound frequency increases, so does the germination rate.

30. C) The frequency of sound

The variable manipulated in the experiment was the sound frequency.

31. D) 15%

The 15% sugar concentration resulted in the highest viscosity (4 cps).

32. B) It increases

As the sugar concentration increases, so does the viscosity of the solution.

33. C) The viscosity of the solution

The variable measured in the experiment was the viscosity of the solution.

34. D) 3 ppm

The chlorine concentration of 3 ppm resulted in the lowest number of bacteria (10 CFU/ml).

35. A) It decreases

As the chlorine concentration increases, the number of bacteria decreases.

36. B) Chlorine concentration

The variable manipulated in the experiment was the chlorine concentration.

37. B) Earth

The soil surface resulted in the highest decomposition rate (25%).

38. B) It increases

The soil surface allowed the highest rate of decomposition of organic matter.

39. C) The type of surface

The variable manipulated in the experiment was the type of surface.

40. D) 0.1057 gal

0.1057 gal of water resulted in the highest algae biomass production (0.7055 oz).

Chapter 10: Analyze Your Practice Test Results

In this chapter, you will learn brief, but forceful and practical recommendations, to know how to analyze the results and, based on this, make adjustments and improve your plan to prepare.

Identify Strengths and Weaknesses

To do this, you must take a meticulous and detailed approach allowing you to break down every aspect of your performance. Check all the incorrect questions and determine whether the error was due to a lack of understanding of the concept, a misinterpretation, or an oversight. If you made a mistake because you didn't fully understand the underlying concept, it means there is a weakness in that specific area.

Likewise, examine the correct ones but in which you doubted or took more time than necessary. Even if you were right, the doubt would indicate a superficial understanding of the topic. With this, you will know where to reinforce your knowledge to gain more confidence. Write them down and review why you hesitated.

The time you took to answer each question is another key indicator. If you took longer than expected to solve certain sections, this would suggest a weakness in the speed and efficiency with which you process. Write down how long it took you to answer each one and look for patterns in your management. If you discovered it took you longer to answer those that require complex calculations, there could be a weakness in the speed of resolution.

Review the explanations of the correct answers to understand why they are the best option and verify the logic behind them. If you realize you got a question right through intuition rather than solid knowledge, this indicates areas where your understanding could be deeper. This detailed analysis helps you build a stronger foundation of knowledge and keeps your thinking process on track.

Reflect on your emotional and mental state. Note whether there were times when you felt anxious or insecure and whether they coincided with an increase in the number of mistakes. This way, you will know whether or not you should work on stress management techniques and develop strategies to stay focused.

Consider how you approach interpreting complex or ambiguous questions. Practice breaking them down into more manageable parts and look for contextual clues.

Compare your results from different practice tests to get a more complete view of your strengths and weaknesses. If you see improvements in certain areas or persistent patterns, it will give you a clear idea of your progress.

Ask for feedback from teachers, tutors, or classmates. Sometimes an outside perspective for noticing things you hadn't noticed and for receiving advice on how to improve. A tutor is trained to provide specific techniques.

If you find certain areas remain problematic, look for additional explanations, educational videos, or materials addressing those topics in depth. Practice with different types of resources to understand the concepts from multiple angles and reinforce your knowledge.

Maintain an attitude of continuous learning and self-assessment. Continue to evaluate your progress and adjust your strategies as necessary.

Review Focused on Your Scores

To conduct a focused review based on your ACT scores, break down each section of the test to get a detailed understanding of your performance. Analyze each section individually, focusing on the specific areas tested on the test.

Take note of your raw and scaled scores. The raw scores represent the total number of correct questions in each section. The scaled results adjust these numbers to be comparable across different versions of the test. This adjustment is important because the scaled scores reflect your true performance relative to others.

Look at your scores in each section, and within each one identify the specific subcategories. In math, you could separate problems into algebra, geometry, and trigonometry. This categorization helps to see your overall score in the section and how you performed in each specific subarea.

After breaking down your scores, focus on trends. If you notice your performance is high in algebra but low in geometry, this tells you where you might need more practice or revision. This detailed assessment gives you a clear picture of your proficiency and those areas requiring additional attention. If you have taken several practice tests, compare your scores on each one to see if there are improvements or if certain question types continue to present challenges.

As you conduct this analysis, compare it to the admission requirements of the colleges you plan to apply to. Research the average scores of the students admitted to them and compare them with your results. It gives you a clear idea of how much more you need to improve to achieve your academic goals.

Evaluate the consistency of your performance. If you have fluctuations in your scores between different sections or question types, it is an indicator of your overall preparation. If you find that they vary a lot, it could be a sign that you need to work on stabilizing through more consistent practice.

Keep in mind the relative difficulty of the questions. If your errors are concentrated on those at the beginning, in the middle, or at the end of the section, those at the end are usually more difficult and require a higher level of skill and concentration. If you find you have more errors on these, it tells you that you need to improve your mental stamina and your ability to maintain concentration throughout the test.

Adjust Your Study Plan

To tune it effectively, you must make modifications based on your performance and specific needs. Review the balance of your time. If you have been spending more time on a specific section but do not see improvements, redistribute your time. If you notice spending an hour a day on mathematics is not producing the expected results, divide it into two shorter sessions focused on different subtopics.

If your sessions are long but unproductive, reduce the duration and increase the frequency so you can maintain concentration and absorb information better. Implement active learning techniques, such as teaching concepts to another person or creating concept maps, to improve your retention of the material.

Schedule specific sessions to review previous concepts, not just to learn new ones. So, the learning will stay fresh. Spend the last 10–15 minutes of each session reviewing previous material. After each one, take a few minutes to reflect on what you learned and how you felt. Write down your observations and adjust based on these reflections.

If certain resources are not effective, replace them with others that better fit your learning style. Do not limit yourself to a single type of resource; diversify to find what works best for you.

Implement a rotation of topics, rotating between different topics or sections each day or each session. This technique keeps you active and engaged, you will be able to see connections between different areas of the test.

While you don't need to redefine your goals, make sure they remain relevant and achievable by looking if your progress is faster or slower than expected and adjusting your expectations and deadlines accordingly.

Use a journal or spreadsheet to keep a detailed record of your sessions, including what you studied, how much time you spent, and any other observations. This monitoring allows you to identify patterns and make informed adjustments to your plan.

Another adjustment that could be very helpful is to incorporate deliberate practice into your studying. Instead of spending more time studying, focus on practicing the areas where you find the most difficulties, such as doing more challenging problems, focusing on specific types of questions, or reviewing concepts you don't fully understand.

These continuous adjustments will help you optimize your plan, so each session is as productive and effective as possible.

Part V:
The Last Stretch

Chapter 11: The Week Before the Test

This one will be a decisive week, in which you must work on your well-being, and review each aspect you have learned, without oversaturating yourself. This is why I invite you to implement these recommendations.

Last-Minute Tips and Strategies

Keep these easy-to-apply actions in mind:

Review Summaries and Keynotes

This week is important to refresh what is most important, so the fundamental concepts are clear and fresh. Begin your review by dedicating each day to a specific topic and dividing the material into manageable chunks. This avoids overload and allows for more effective review. As you review, use techniques like reading aloud to improve information retention.

Review Common Mistakes and How to Avoid Them

Reviewing and understanding why they occurred is key to avoiding repeating them. Analyze previous practice tests and write down the most common types of errors. Once you have a list, reflect on the causes. If they were due to misinterpretation of questions, calculation problems, or lapses in concentration, practice with questions similar to those caused problems. Read them very carefully to verify you understand what is being asked. By doing this, you will be able to understand the requirements before answering and develop an effective strategy to avoid similar errors. Reflect after each practice session and evaluate if you have improved in the problematic aspects you identified. If they persist, look for additional resources.

Read High Scoring Essay Examples

These essays show how an effective argument is structured, how ideas are developed coherently, and how concrete examples are used to support claims. By observing how others have approached similar topics, you can discover techniques and strategies you could apply in your essay.

Choose high-quality examples and essays that have received perfect or near-perfect scores. Pay attention to how they are structured, the clarity of the argument, and the way the evidence is presented. Look at the many topics and writing styles to get a broad view of what is considered a good essay. Analyze how the author introduces the topic, develops the points, and concludes convincingly. You will notice they present and explore ideas in depth, demonstrating critical and analytical thinking.

Pay attention to grammar and writing style, how authors avoid common mistakes, and how they structure their sentences to maintain flow and the reader's interest. Take note of the techniques you find most effective and think about how you could incorporate them into your writing style.

Make Flashcards with Key Concepts

They are an effective tool to review and memorize key concepts in the last week of preparation. They serve to focus on the most important points quickly and repetitively, which is ideal for consolidating knowledge. You just have to write a concept or question on one side of the card and the definition or answer on the other. In mathematics, you could write important formulas and on the other side, their applications. In English, you might have grammar rules, examples of correct and incorrect usage, and definitions of rhetorical terms. Review your cards several times daily, at short intervals, to maximize review effectiveness. Take them with you and review them at any time, even taking advantage of small breaks during the day.

Review Essential Mathematical Formulas

The last week is ideal for reinforcing this knowledge, particularly focusing on formulas used most frequently to solve problems efficiently. For example, the quadratic formula is essential for finding the roots of quadratic equations. It is also important to remember the area of a circle, πr^2, and the circumference, $2 \pi r$. Don't forget the volume formulas for geometric figures such as the volume of a cylinder, $\pi r^2 h$, and of a cone, $1/3 \pi r^2 h$.

Trigonometric formulas, such as sine, cosine, and tangent, are important, along with basic trigonometric identities such as $\sin^2 \theta + \cos^2 \theta = 1$. That of the Pythagorean theorem, $a^2 + b^2 = c^2$, is necessary for geometry problems. For the slope of a line, $(y_2 - y_1) / (x_2 - x_1)$, it is important for coordinate problems. Practice some problems and use them to strengthen your memory and ability to apply them.

Prepare Everything You Need for the Test

The first thing is to have your ID, such as a driver's license or a school ID card, as it is an essential requirement to enter the test center. You will need your admission ticket, which you should print and have ready.

Don't forget to bring several sharp No. 2 pencils, a good quality eraser, and a working ACT-approved calculator with charged batteries or carry spare batteries. A wristwatch, without alarm functions, will help you manage your time, since many centers do not allow the use of watches with alarms or smartwatches.

Pack a bottle of water and some healthy snacks to consume during breaks to stay hydrated and energized. Plan your route to the test center and estimate how long it will take you to get there, taking into account traffic or possible delays. Check the night before that everything is ready and in place so that the morning of the test is as smooth as possible.

Mental and Physical Preparation

You should not focus only on your training; you must be ready with a healthy, balanced mind and full physical condition. Therefore, I offer you these recommendations.

Sleep at Least 8 Hours at Night

A restful sleep of at least 8 hours per night improves concentration and mood. During this period, the brain processes information and consolidates memory.

To get a good rest, go to bed and get up at the same time every day to regulate your biological clock. Avoid using electronic devices at least an hour before bed, as the blue light from screens interferes with the production of melatonin, the hormone that regulates sleep, opt for relaxing activities such as reading a book or taking a hot bath. Create a pleasant environment so that your room is dark, quiet, and at a comfortable temperature.

Perform Deep Breathing Exercises

These exercises reduce stress and anxiety while increasing the oxygen supply to the brain, which helps maintain clarity:

Diaphragmatic breathing

1. Place one hand on your chest and the other on your abdomen.

2. Inhale through your nose, filling your abdomen and allowing the hand on your abdomen to rise.

3. Make sure the hand on your chest moves as little as possible.

4. Exhale through your mouth, feeling the hand on your abdomen lower.

5. Repeat this breath 5 to 10 times.

6. Focus on the sensation of filling and emptying your abdomen.

7. Maintain a slow and steady pace throughout the exercise.

Breathing 4-7-8

1. Inhale through your nose for 4 seconds.

2. Hold your breath for 7 seconds.

3. Exhale through your mouth for 8 seconds.

4. Inhale through your nose and repeat the cycle.

5. Perform this exercise 4 to 8 times.

6. Focus on counting the seconds.

Maintain a Balanced Diet

A diet rich in fruits, vegetables, lean proteins, and whole grains provides the essential nutrients your brain and body need to function optimally. Eat foods rich in antioxidants such as blueberries and walnuts to improve brain function and protect cells from oxidative stress. Include proteins like eggs, chicken, and fish, which help maintain energy and focus throughout the day. Avoid processed and sugary foods as they cause spikes and dips in energy levels, affecting concentration and performance. Healthy fats, such as those found in avocado and walnuts, are beneficial for the brain and cognition. Stay well-hydrated by drinking enough water throughout the day. Limit caffeine and energy drinks because they cause anxiety and affect sleep.

Practice Yoga or Light Stretches

These exercises improve circulation, increase flexibility, and help release tension built up in the body:

Child's pose (Balasana)

1. Sit back on your heels.

2. Lean forward and extend your arms in front of you.

3. Rest your forehead on the floor.

4. Hold this position and breathe deeply.

5. Relax in this posture for 1–2 minutes.

Downward-facing dog pose (Adho Mukha Svanasana)

1. Get into a tabletop position with your hands and knees on the floor.

2. Lift your hips up and back.

3. Keep your heels on the floor and your arms extended.

4. Align your head between your arms.

5. Hold the posture for 1–2 minutes.

Warrior pose II (Virabhadrasana II)

1. Take a big step forward with one foot.

2. Turn your back foot outward at a 90-degree angle.

3. Extend your arms to your sides, parallel to the floor.

4. Bend your front knee, keeping your knee in line with your ankle.

5. Hold this position for 1–2 minutes; then, switch sides.

Neck stretch

1. Sit or stand with your back straight.

2. Tilt your head to one side, bringing your ear to your shoulder.

3. Hold the position for 20–30 seconds.

4. Switch sides and repeat.

5. Perform this stretch 2–3 times on each side.

Shoulder stretch

1. Cross one arm over your chest.

2. Use your other hand to press your arm toward your body.

3. Hold the position for 20–30 seconds.

4. Switch arms and repeat.

5. Perform this stretch 2–3 times on each side.

Lower back stretch

1. Lie on your back with your knees bent.

2. Hug your knees and bring them towards your chest.

3. Hold the position for 20–30 seconds.

4. Release and repeat.

5. Perform this stretch 2–3 times.

Listen to soothing music

Soft instrumental music, such as the piano or violin, is beneficial because it avoids distractions from the lyrics and promotes deep relaxation. When listening to relaxing music, the body responds by slowing the heart rate and reducing cortisol levels, the stress hormone.

During study sessions, choose soft tunes that help you stay focused without distracting you. Experiment with different genres and styles to make you feel centered and improve your mood.

Chapter 12: Test Day and Beyond

Test day can be one of the most important days of your academic life. Being prepared and knowing what to expect will make a difference.

What to Expect on Test Day

When you wake up, do so with enough time to prepare without rushing; this gives you time to relax, have breakfast, and get to the test center without stress. Consume foods that sustain energy, such as oatmeal, fruits, yogurt, and eggs.

Dress comfortably and in layers, as the temperature in the center may vary. Before leaving home, ensure you have everything you need: your ID, admission ticket, pencils, eraser, calculator, water, and snacks. Leave with plenty of time to avoid the stress of arriving late.

When you arrive at the test center, there may be a line to register; please follow the staff's instructions. Once registered, you will be assigned a room where the test will take place. They will give you specific instructions on how to proceed; don't hesitate to ask questions if something is unclear.

You may have to wait a bit before it starts. Use this time to relax and review your strategies, have a positive attitude, and trust in your preparation.

When you are given the test, read the instructions carefully, make sure you understand the format and how to mark your answers, and remember how much time to spend on each section without rushing. If you find a question difficult, don't dwell too long.

Focus on one question at a time. Don't think about the questions you have answered or the ones to come. If you start to feel anxious, use deep breathing techniques to calm yourself.

Breaks between sections are important; use them to stretch, drink water, and have a snack if needed. Avoid discussing answers or questions with others during breaks, as this could distract you.

In the end, take the time to double-check everything. Look for transcription errors and ensure that you have answered all questions. Don't leave any blank, as there is no penalty for guessing.

After handing in your test, leave the room calmly. Congratulate yourself for completing it, and remember you did everything you could to prepare.

Once at home, relax and give yourself a well-deserved rest. Engage in activities you enjoy, to unwind and relieve the tension of the day. It's normal to feel a mix of emotions, from relief to nervousness. Accept these feelings and remember results are only part of your academic journey.

After the Test: Score Interpretation and Next Steps

After completing the test, it may be a relief to know your effort and dedication have been tested, but this is not the end. Now you understand how to interpret your practice test scores, apply those same steps here to understand your results on the actual ACT.

Upon receiving them, take some time to review them. After interpreting them, it is time to consider the next steps.

First, reflect on how these scores align with your academic and career goals. If you met or exceeded your expected scores, congratulate yourself and consider how these results position you in your college applications. If you didn't reach your goals, don't be discouraged; this is a time to evaluate your options and plan your next moves.

If they are satisfactory and meet the requirements of the universities you are applying to, focus on the application process. Research application deadlines and have all the necessary documents. It is the time to gather letters of recommendation, write admissions essays, and fill out forms; earlier chapters provide recommendations for these tasks.

If your scores do not meet your expectations, you have several options. You could opt to retake the ACT; many students do this more than once to improve their scores. If you decide to retake the test, analyze the areas where improvement is needed and focus on them.

It's also beneficial to consult with an academic advisor or mentor. They can provide valuable insights into your next steps and help you explore other colleges and programs that better suit your current score while aligning with your academic goals.

Move forward with confidence. University is a stage in your educational journey, and there are many ways to achieve your goals. Another option is education at institutions that have more flexible admission policies. Many universities and community colleges offer excellent programs that serve as a stepping stone to higher education. A year or two at a community college could give you a solid foundation, allowing you to transfer to a four-year university with a bonus of experience and academic credits.

If you decide not to retake the ACT, focus on improving other aspects of your academic profile. Participate in advanced courses, workshops, or certifications that align with your interests and professional goals.

Remember, the college admissions process is not a race against time; be patient, maintain a positive mindset, and focus on the opportunities ahead. Your path to higher education is full of possibilities; use your scores as a guide to make informed and strategic decisions.

Conclusion

Reaching the end of this guide is an accomplishment and marks the beginning of an exciting stage in your life. Then, with all the strategies, techniques, and knowledge acquired, you are better prepared to tackle the test.

The learning process does not stop with the test; it is a continuous journey leading to new opportunities. Maintain the discipline and resilience you have developed during this preparation.

Your dedication to this process has been an investment in yourself. Now, trust in your abilities and the work you have done.

Made in the USA
Coppell, TX
31 May 2025

50129265R00151